MALWARE ANALYSIS

DIGITAL FORENSICS, CYBERSECURITY, AND INCIDENT RESPONSE

4 BOOKS IN 1

BOOK 1
INTRODUCTION TO MALWARE ANALYSIS AND DIGITAL FORENSICS FOR CYBERSECURITY

BOOK 2
MALWARE DETECTION AND ANALYSIS IN CYBERSECURITY: A PRACTICAL APPROACH

BOOK 3
ADVANCED CYBERSECURITY THREAT ANALYSIS AND INCIDENT RESPONSE

BOOK 4
EXPERT MALWARE ANALYSIS AND DIGITAL FORENSICS: MASTERING CYBERSECURITY INCIDENT RESPONSE

ROB BOTWRIGHT

Published by Rob Botwright
Library of Congress Cataloging-in-Publication Data
ISBN 978-1-83938-531-5
Cover design by Rizzo

Disclaimer

The contents of this book are based on extensive research and the best available historical sources. However, the author and publisher make no claims, promises, or guarantees about the accuracy, completeness, or adequacy of the information contained herein. The information in this book is provided on an "as is" basis, and the author and publisher disclaim any and all liability for any errors, omissions, or inaccuracies in the information or for any actions taken in reliance on such information. The opinions and views expressed in this book are those of the author and do not necessarily reflect the official policy or position of any organization or individual mentioned in this book. Any reference to specific people, places, or events is intended only to provide historical context and is not intended to defame or malign any group, individual, or entity. The information in this book is intended for educational and entertainment purposes only. It is not intended to be a substitute for professional advice or judgment. Readers are encouraged to conduct their own research and to seek professional advice where appropriate. Every effort has been made to obtain necessary permissions and acknowledgments for all images and other copyrighted material used in this book. Any errors or omissions in this regard are unintentional, and the author and publisher will correct them in future editions.

TABLE OF CONTENTS – BOOK 1 - INTRODUCTION TO MALWARE ANALYSIS AND DIGITAL FORENSICS FOR CYBERSECURITY

TABLE OF CONTENTS – BOOK 2 - MALWARE DETECTION AND ANALYSIS IN CYBERSECURITY: A PRACTICAL APPROACH

TABLE OF CONTENTS – BOOK 3 - ADVANCED CYBERSECURITY THREAT ANALYSIS AND INCIDENT RESPONSE

TABLE OF CONTENTS – BOOK 4 - EXPERT MALWARE ANALYSIS AND DIGITAL FORENSICS: MASTERING CYBERSECURITY INCIDENT RESPONSE

Introduction

In an age dominated by technology and the interconnectedness of our digital lives, the guardians of our virtual realm face an unending challenge. Cyber threats loom large, evolving into formidable adversaries that constantly test the limits of our defenses. It is in this ever-shifting battleground of the digital world that the book bundle "Malware Analysis, Digital Forensics, Cybersecurity, and Incident Response" emerges as an indispensable guide.

This comprehensive bundle, comprised of four distinct volumes, delves into the heart of cybersecurity, offering a holistic understanding of the intricate and dynamic landscape of cyber threats and defenses. Each book, with its unique focus and depth of knowledge, equips readers with the tools and insights needed to navigate the complexities of modern cybersecurity.

In Book 1, "Introduction to Malware Analysis and Digital Forensics for Cybersecurity," we embark on our journey by laying a solid foundation. Here, we explore the very essence of malware, dissecting its anatomy and understanding its behavior. We delve into the realm of digital forensics, uncovering the techniques used to uncover hidden digital evidence. This introductory volume equips readers with essential knowledge, ensuring they are well-prepared for the challenges that lie ahead.

Book 2, "Malware Detection and Analysis in Cybersecurity: A Practical Approach," takes us further into the practical aspects of malware defense. With a focus on real-world applications, this book introduces various malware detection approaches, from the conventional signature-based methods to the more sophisticated heuristic and behavioral analysis. Readers gain a hands-on understanding of how to detect, analyze, and respond effectively to malware threats.

As we progress to Book 3, "Advanced Cybersecurity Threat Analysis and Incident Response," we ascend to a new level of expertise. Here, we explore advanced threat analysis techniques and delve into the minds of sophisticated adversaries. The importance of threat intelligence and proactive threat hunting becomes evident as we prepare readers to confront evolving cyber threats head-on.

Finally, in Book 4, "Expert Malware Analysis and Digital Forensics: Mastering Cybersecurity Incident Response," we reach the pinnacle of our journey. We unravel the intricacies of malware analysis, master memory forensics, and become adept at incident response. This book equips readers with the skills and knowledge needed to dissect malware with surgical precision and respond decisively to security incidents.

Throughout this bundle, we emphasize the indispensable role of collaboration and communication within the cybersecurity community. Effective teamwork, both within organizations and across the industry, is key to mitigating cyber threats and fortifying our collective digital defenses.

As we embark on this comprehensive exploration of malware analysis, digital forensics, cybersecurity, and incident response, we invite readers to join us on a journey through the depths of cyberspace. In the face of relentless cyber threats, knowledge is our greatest weapon, and it is this knowledge that this book bundle seeks to impart.

The digital realm is constantly evolving, and the defenders of cyberspace must evolve with it. With each page turned and each concept grasped, readers will become better equipped to safeguard our digital future. Welcome to the world of "Malware Analysis, Digital Forensics, Cybersecurity, and Incident Response" – your guide to mastering the art of cyber defense in an age of relentless threats.

BOOK 1
INTRODUCTION TO MALWARE ANALYSIS AND DIGITAL
FORENSICS FOR CYBERSECURITY

ROB BOTWRIGHT

Chapter 1: The Cybersecurity Landscape

Next, let's discuss emerging cyber threats. In the ever-evolving landscape of cybersecurity, staying informed about the latest threats is crucial for individuals and organizations alike.

These emerging threats often exploit new vulnerabilities or leverage innovative attack vectors. As technology continues to advance, so do the capabilities of cybercriminals and threat actors. It's a constant game of cat and mouse between security professionals and those seeking to breach security measures.

One notable category of emerging threats is related to the Internet of Things (IoT). With the proliferation of connected devices, from smart thermostats to industrial control systems, there are more entry points for cyberattacks. Hackers can target these devices to gain access to networks and potentially cause significant damage or data breaches.

Moreover, cloud computing has become a vital part of modern business operations. While the cloud offers numerous benefits, it also introduces new security challenges. Misconfigured cloud settings or inadequate access controls can lead to data exposure or unauthorized access.

Ransomware attacks have also evolved, becoming more sophisticated and damaging. Attackers now engage in double extortion, not only encrypting victims' data but also threatening to release sensitive information if a ransom is not paid. This tactic increases the pressure on organizations to meet attackers' demands.

Supply chain attacks have gained prominence in recent years as well. Instead of directly targeting a company's systems, attackers compromise trusted vendors or service providers, enabling them to infiltrate the target organization's network indirectly. This tactic can have far-reaching consequences, impacting multiple organizations within the supply chain.

Nation-state-sponsored cyberattacks remain a significant concern. Governments and state-sponsored groups conduct cyber espionage, cyberwarfare, and cybercriminal activities to achieve their strategic objectives. Such attacks can target critical infrastructure, government institutions, or private corporations, posing substantial risks to national security and the global economy.

Emerging threats aren't limited to technology. Social engineering attacks, such as phishing and spear-phishing, continue to be effective methods for gaining unauthorized access to systems or compromising user credentials. Attackers craft convincing messages that deceive individuals into taking actions that benefit the attacker, like clicking on malicious links or downloading infected files.

To combat these threats effectively, organizations must adopt a proactive approach to cybersecurity. This involves continuous monitoring, threat intelligence sharing, and the implementation of robust security measures. It's also crucial to educate employees about security best practices and the importance of remaining vigilant against social engineering attacks.

As a part of this proactive approach, organizations should regularly update and patch their systems to address known vulnerabilities. Vulnerability management programs help identify and prioritize patches based on the potential impact of an exploit.

Network segmentation and access controls can limit the lateral movement of attackers within a network, reducing the potential damage in case of a breach. Additionally, the use of multi-factor authentication (MFA) adds an extra layer of security by requiring multiple forms of verification before granting access.

Threat intelligence feeds and services provide organizations with valuable information about emerging threats and the tactics, techniques, and procedures (TTPs) of cyber adversaries. This information enables organizations to tailor their defenses and response strategies accordingly.

In summary, the world of cybersecurity is in a constant state of flux, with emerging threats posing significant challenges to individuals and organizations. Understanding these threats, adopting proactive security measures, and staying informed about the latest developments in the cybersecurity landscape are essential steps in defending against cyberattacks.

Understanding the importance of cybersecurity awareness is crucial in today's digital age. It's not just a concern for IT professionals or security experts; it's a responsibility that extends to every individual who uses digital technology.

The digital realm has become an integral part of our lives, from personal communication to business operations and critical infrastructure. With this increasing dependence on technology, the risks associated with cyber threats have grown exponentially. Cyberattacks can have severe consequences, ranging from financial losses and data breaches to reputational damage and even threats to national security. It's not just about protecting sensitive information; it's about safeguarding our way of life in an interconnected world.

Cybercriminals are constantly evolving, devising new techniques and exploiting vulnerabilities in software, hardware, and human behavior. They target individuals, organizations, and governments alike. The ubiquity of the internet and the sheer volume of connected devices provide ample opportunities for these adversaries to exploit.

To address these challenges effectively, we need to recognize that cybersecurity is everyone's responsibility. It's not a problem that can be solved solely by the efforts of cybersecurity professionals or IT departments. Cybersecurity awareness begins with understanding the risks and threats that exist in the digital space. It involves recognizing the different forms of cyberattacks, such as phishing, malware, ransomware, and social engineering. Awareness helps individuals identify suspicious activities and potential threats, enabling them to take proactive measures to protect themselves and their digital assets.

Furthermore, cybersecurity awareness extends to understanding the importance of strong passwords and the significance of regular updates and patches. Neglecting these aspects can leave vulnerabilities that cybercriminals are quick to exploit.

An essential aspect of cybersecurity awareness is recognizing the value of personal information. Our digital presence, including social media profiles and online accounts, contains a wealth of personal data. Protecting this information is not just about privacy; it's about preventing identity theft and cybercrimes that can have devastating consequences.

Businesses and organizations also bear a significant responsibility in promoting cybersecurity awareness among their employees. Training and education programs should be in place to ensure that staff members are informed about best practices and the latest threats.

Employees play a vital role in an organization's cybersecurity posture. They are often the first line of defense against social engineering attacks like phishing. A well-informed employee is less likely to fall victim to such tactics. Moreover, businesses must implement robust cybersecurity policies and practices. These include access controls, network security measures, data encryption, and incident response plans. Regular security audits and assessments can help identify weaknesses and ensure that protective measures are up to date.

The consequences of a cybersecurity breach can be financially crippling for a business. Beyond immediate financial losses, there are often long-term impacts, such as damaged reputation and loss of customer trust. Cybersecurity awareness, coupled with robust cybersecurity measures, can significantly reduce the risk of such breaches.

Government bodies also play a crucial role in promoting cybersecurity awareness and setting standards for digital safety. Cybersecurity regulations and frameworks provide guidelines for organizations to follow, helping to create a safer digital environment for all.

Collaboration is key in the fight against cyber threats. Public-private partnerships, information sharing, and threat intelligence exchange are essential elements in building a collective defense against cyber adversaries.

Ultimately, the importance of cybersecurity awareness cannot be overstated. It's about safeguarding our digital lives, protecting our personal information, and ensuring the security and resilience of our critical infrastructure.

Cybersecurity awareness is not a one-time effort; it's an ongoing commitment. It requires staying informed about the evolving threat landscape, being vigilant in our online activities, and taking proactive steps to mitigate risks.

In today's interconnected world, cybersecurity is a shared responsibility. It's a responsibility that falls on individuals, organizations, and governments alike. By raising awareness and taking collective action, we can better defend against cyber threats and create a safer digital environment for everyone.

Chapter 2: Understanding Malicious Software

In the vast landscape of malware, one of the most well-known and commonly encountered types are viruses. These malicious programs, named after their biological counterparts, share some similarities with their natural counterparts, specifically in their ability to spread and infect. Viruses are designed to attach themselves to legitimate files or programs, essentially embedding their malicious code within these innocent-looking carriers.

When an infected file or program is executed, the virus is activated, and it can then replicate itself and spread to other files, often throughout the entire computer system. This replication and spread mimic the behavior of biological viruses, which can propagate from host to host.

Unlike viruses, worms are standalone malicious programs that do not need to attach themselves to other files or programs to spread. They are capable of self-replication and can propagate independently by exploiting vulnerabilities in networked devices or software.

Worms can rapidly infect numerous computers across networks, making them particularly dangerous. They often target vulnerabilities in operating systems, email clients, or network services, taking advantage of security weaknesses to gain access and replicate.

A key distinction between viruses and worms is that viruses require user interaction to initiate their code, such as running an infected program or opening an infected email attachment, while worms can spread autonomously once they exploit a vulnerability.

Both viruses and worms can cause significant harm to computer systems and networks. They can corrupt or delete files, steal sensitive data, disrupt system operations, and provide unauthorized access to malicious actors. The impact of these malware types can range from minor inconveniences to major security breaches.

To protect against viruses and worms, it's essential to employ robust antivirus and antimalware solutions that can detect and quarantine infected files or remove malicious code. Regular software updates and security patches are also crucial in preventing these malware types, as they often exploit known vulnerabilities that are patched by software vendors.

Furthermore, user education plays a critical role in defense against viruses and worms. Individuals should exercise caution when opening email attachments or downloading files from untrusted sources, as these are common infection vectors.

Maintaining strong password practices and practicing good cyber hygiene, such as avoiding suspicious websites and email links, can go a long way in mitigating the risks associated with these malware types.

It's worth noting that the lines between different types of malware are not always clear-cut. Some malware can exhibit characteristics of both viruses and worms, making classification a challenge. Additionally, the landscape of malware is continually evolving, with new variants and hybrid forms emerging regularly.

In summary, viruses and worms represent two distinct but related categories of malware. Viruses attach themselves to legitimate files or programs and require user interaction to initiate their malicious code, while worms are standalone programs that can self-replicate and spread independently, often exploiting network vulnerabilities. Protecting against these malware types requires a combination of robust security measures, including antivirus software, software updates, user education, and strong cybersecurity practices.

Now, let's delve into two other significant types of malware: Trojans and Ransomware. First, let's explore Trojans.

Trojans are malicious programs named after the famous wooden horse from ancient Greek mythology. Similar to the deceptive nature of the legendary horse, Trojans disguise themselves as legitimate software or files, tricking users into unknowingly installing them. Unlike viruses and worms, Trojans don't replicate or spread independently; instead, they rely on social engineering tactics to infiltrate systems.

Once inside a computer or network, Trojans can carry out a variety of malicious actions. They may create backdoors, providing unauthorized access to cybercriminals. Some Trojans are designed to steal sensitive data, such as login credentials or financial information, while others might serve as a delivery mechanism for additional malware.

Ransomware, on the other hand, is a particularly insidious type of malware that has gained notoriety in recent years. This malicious software is aptly named because it "kidnaps" a victim's data, encrypts it, and then demands a ransom in exchange for the decryption key. Ransomware attacks can be devastating for individuals and organizations alike.

The impact of ransomware goes beyond the immediate financial demand. It can disrupt critical operations, lead to data loss, and result in significant downtime. In some cases, victims may choose to pay the ransom, but there's no guarantee that they will receive the decryption key, and it may encourage further criminal activity.

Ransomware comes in various forms, including encrypting ransomware, which locks files or entire systems, and screen-locking ransomware, which prevents users from accessing their devices or data. There are also ransomware-as-a-service (RaaS) offerings, which allow cybercriminals to easily launch ransomware attacks without significant technical expertise.

The delivery methods for Trojans and ransomware can vary. They often arrive as email attachments, malicious links, or disguised downloads from untrusted sources. Social engineering plays a crucial role in tricking victims into opening these malicious payloads, emphasizing the importance of user education and awareness.

Protecting against Trojans and ransomware requires a multi-layered approach. Robust antivirus and anti-malware solutions can detect and block these threats.

Regular software updates and patch management help eliminate vulnerabilities that malware can exploit.

Backing up data is also essential. Regularly backing up files to offline or secure cloud storage ensures that even if data is encrypted by ransomware, you have a clean copy to restore. However, it's crucial to maintain secure backup practices to prevent ransomware from infecting backups.

User education remains a key defense. Training individuals to recognize phishing emails, avoid suspicious downloads, and exercise caution when clicking on links can significantly reduce the risk of falling victim to Trojans and ransomware.

Additionally, some security solutions employ behavior-based detection techniques, which can identify and stop malware based on its actions rather than relying solely on known signatures.

Lastly, having an incident response plan in place is critical. In the unfortunate event of a malware infection, organizations need a well-defined plan to contain, eradicate, and recover from the incident.

In summary, Trojans and ransomware represent two prominent and dangerous categories of malware. Trojans rely on deception to infiltrate systems and can perform various malicious actions, while ransomware encrypts data and demands a ransom for its release. Defending against these threats requires a combination of technical defenses, user education, secure backup practices, and incident response preparedness.

Chapter 3: Digital Forensics Essentials

Let's explore the role of digital forensics in investigations. Digital forensics is a specialized field within cybersecurity and law enforcement that focuses on the collection, analysis, and preservation of digital evidence to investigate cybercrimes and other illicit activities.

In today's digital age, digital devices and technology are integral to our personal and professional lives. We use smartphones, computers, tablets, and other digital devices to communicate, work, shop, and conduct various activities online. This increased digital footprint has also created new opportunities for criminals to engage in cybercrimes, ranging from hacking and identity theft to fraud and cyber espionage.

Digital forensics plays a vital role in uncovering evidence related to these cybercrimes. It involves the systematic examination of digital devices and electronic data to identify, preserve, and analyze information that can be used in legal proceedings. This evidence can be critical in both criminal and civil cases, helping to establish facts, attribute actions to specific individuals or entities, and support investigations.

Digital forensics encompasses a wide range of activities and techniques. These include data acquisition, where investigators gather digital evidence from various sources such as computers, mobile devices, servers, and cloud storage. The process must be conducted carefully to ensure that the integrity of the evidence is maintained, so it remains admissible in court.

Once data is acquired, digital forensic analysts employ a variety of tools and methods to examine it. This examination can reveal a wealth of information, including user activities, communications, file access, and even deleted data. Analysts use specialized software and hardware to recover and analyze digital artifacts.

One essential aspect of digital forensics is data preservation. Investigators must ensure that evidence is protected from tampering, loss, or destruction. This involves creating forensic copies of data that are kept in a secure, unaltered state for analysis while maintaining the original evidence's integrity.

The forensic analysis process can uncover a range of digital evidence, including emails, documents, chat logs, browsing history, and more. This evidence can be used to reconstruct events, identify potential suspects, and provide a timeline of activities. Digital forensic experts are often called upon to testify in court as expert witnesses to explain their findings.

Digital forensics is not limited to criminal investigations. It is also valuable in civil cases, internal corporate investigations, and regulatory compliance. For example, in the corporate world, digital forensics can help uncover evidence of employee misconduct, intellectual property theft, or data breaches.

In addition to traditional digital devices like computers and mobile phones, digital forensics extends to emerging technologies. This includes investigating IoT

(Internet of Things) devices, wearable technology, and cloud-based services, which are increasingly relevant in modern investigations.

Moreover, as technology evolves, so do the challenges in digital forensics. Encrypted data, secure messaging apps, and anonymization techniques pose hurdles for investigators seeking to access critical evidence. As a result, digital forensic experts must continuously update their skills and techniques to keep pace with technological advancements.

The field of digital forensics is interdisciplinary, involving aspects of computer science, law enforcement, legal proceedings, and cybersecurity. It requires a deep understanding of both technology and the legal framework surrounding digital evidence. Investigators must follow strict ethical guidelines and legal procedures to ensure the admissibility of digital evidence in court.

In summary, digital forensics is a critical component of modern investigations, providing the means to uncover digital evidence and support legal proceedings. Its role extends beyond criminal cases to civil litigation, corporate investigations, and regulatory compliance. As technology continues to advance, the importance of digital forensics in the realm of cybersecurity and law enforcement will only continue to grow.

Let's delve into the critical topic of legal and ethical considerations in the field of digital forensics. Digital forensics, as we discussed earlier, involves the systematic examination of digital devices and electronic data to collect and analyze evidence for use in legal proceedings. In the process of conducting digital investigations, professionals must adhere to a set of legal and ethical principles to ensure the integrity and admissibility of the evidence they uncover.

One of the foundational principles in digital forensics is the need for a lawful basis to conduct an investigation. This means that investigators must have the appropriate legal authorization, such as a search warrant or court order, to access and examine digital evidence. Without legal authorization, the collection of digital evidence may be deemed illegal and inadmissible in court.

Furthermore, investigators must be aware of the scope and limitations of their legal authority. For example, a search warrant may specify the devices or data that can be examined and the timeframe within which the investigation must occur. Deviating from these parameters can raise legal and ethical concerns.

Privacy considerations are paramount in digital forensics. Investigators must balance their duty to collect evidence with the rights of individuals to privacy. This includes respecting Fourth Amendment protections against unreasonable searches and seizures in the United States and similar legal principles in other jurisdictions.

In many cases, digital forensic investigations involve examining personal devices or data belonging to individuals who are not necessarily suspects in a criminal case. In such situations, forensic experts must exercise extreme care to avoid infringing upon the privacy rights of innocent parties.

Another key ethical consideration is the preservation of evidence integrity. Digital evidence is often fragile and susceptible to tampering. Digital forensic experts must follow strict procedures to ensure that evidence remains unaltered and admissible in court. This involves creating forensic copies of data, maintaining a chain of custody, and documenting every step of the examination process.

In addition to legal and privacy concerns, ethical considerations extend to professional conduct. Digital forensic experts are expected to uphold high ethical standards and maintain objectivity in their investigations. They must avoid biases and conflicts of interest that could compromise the integrity of their findings.

Transparency and accountability are crucial aspects of ethical digital forensics. Investigators should be prepared to document and explain their actions, methodologies, and findings in a clear and understandable manner, particularly when presenting evidence in court. This transparency ensures that the legal process remains fair and just.

Furthermore, digital forensic experts should stay up-to-date with evolving laws and regulations related to digital evidence. In the dynamic field of technology, legal standards and requirements can change rapidly. Staying informed about these changes is essential to conducting investigations within the bounds of the law.

Cross-border considerations are increasingly relevant in digital forensics, as evidence and digital devices can transcend national borders. Investigators must be aware of international legal frameworks, such as mutual legal assistance treaties (MLATs), which govern the exchange of evidence between countries. Ensuring compliance with these treaties is essential when conducting international investigations.

Ethical digital forensics also involves a commitment to continuing education and professional development. The field is constantly evolving, with new technologies, encryption methods, and cyber threats emerging regularly. Digital forensic experts must remain adaptable and well-informed to effectively navigate these challenges. Lastly, ethical considerations extend to the responsible handling of sensitive and confidential information. Digital forensic experts often encounter highly sensitive data during their investigations. Safeguarding this information and ensuring its confidentiality is essential to maintaining trust and credibility in the field. In summary, legal and ethical considerations are fundamental to the practice of digital forensics. Adhering to legal requirements, respecting privacy rights, preserving evidence integrity, maintaining professionalism, and staying informed about evolving laws and technologies are all essential components of ethical digital investigations. By upholding these principles, digital forensic experts play a critical role in the pursuit of justice while ensuring that the rights of individuals are protected.

Chapter 4: Tools and Technologies for Analysis

Let's embark on an exploration of the fascinating world of malware analysis tools. These tools are the Swiss Army knives of cybersecurity professionals, enabling them to dissect, understand, and combat malicious software. In this digital age, where cyber threats loom large, malware analysis tools are indispensable weapons in the battle against cybercriminals.

First, it's important to understand what malware analysis is all about. At its core, malware analysis is the process of dissecting and examining malicious software to gain insights into its functionality, behavior, and purpose. This process is akin to dissecting a biological specimen to understand its inner workings, only in the realm of cybersecurity.

Now, let's delve into the primary types of malware analysis: static analysis and dynamic analysis. Static analysis involves examining the malware without executing it. Analysts inspect the code, file structure, and characteristics of the malware to identify potential threats and behaviors. It's like studying the blueprint of a building to understand its design and potential vulnerabilities.

On the other hand, dynamic analysis involves executing the malware in a controlled environment, such as a virtual machine or sandbox. Analysts observe how the malware behaves when it's active, looking for signs of malicious activity like network communications, file modifications, or system changes. Dynamic analysis is like observing a wild animal in its natural habitat to understand its behavior.

Now, let's talk about the essential tools used in malware analysis. Antivirus software is often the first line of defense against malware. While it's not a dedicated malware analysis tool, it plays a crucial role in detecting and quarantining known malware. It's like having a security guard at the entrance of your digital world, checking for threats.

Next, we have disassemblers and decompilers. These tools are used for static analysis, allowing analysts to reverse engineer executable files and scripts to understand their code structure. It's like taking apart a complex machine to see how its various components work together.

Debuggers are another indispensable tool in the malware analyst's arsenal. They allow analysts to step through the code of a program, inspecting its memory and variables in real-time. Debuggers are like detectives at a crime scene, looking for clues and anomalies in the evidence.

Packet analyzers and network sniffers are vital for dynamic analysis. They capture and analyze network traffic generated by malware, helping analysts understand its communication patterns and potential command and control servers. These tools act like eavesdroppers, listening in on conversations between the malware and its handlers.

Sandboxes are isolated environments where malware can be safely executed for dynamic analysis. They provide a controlled space for observing the behavior of malware without risking damage to the host system. Think of sandboxes as secure laboratories where researchers can study dangerous organisms.

Memory analysis tools are essential for examining the volatile memory of a computer or device. Malware often hides in memory to avoid detection, and these tools help uncover hidden processes, code injection, and other malicious artifacts. They are like detectives searching for hidden clues within a crime scene.

YARA is a versatile tool used for creating and matching patterns in files and data streams. Analysts use YARA rules to identify known malware or specific behaviors within code. It's like having a set of specialized search dogs trained to find specific scents.

And let's not forget about automated analysis platforms. These tools use machine learning and behavioral analysis to detect and classify malware automatically. They are like digital security guards patrolling the internet, looking for signs of suspicious activity.

Furthermore, there are tools for analyzing malicious documents, such as PDFs and Office files, which are common vectors for malware delivery. These tools dissect the structure and content of documents to uncover hidden threats.

Code analyzers and profilers help analysts understand the performance and efficiency of malware. They reveal how the code is optimized and where bottlenecks may occur, which can be critical for understanding its impact on a system.

Finally, forensic tools play a crucial role in malware analysis, especially when it comes to incident response and legal investigations. They allow for the collection and preservation of digital evidence, ensuring that findings are admissible in court.

In the world of malware analysis, these tools are the instruments of discovery and defense. They empower cybersecurity professionals to dissect and understand the inner workings of malware, enabling them to develop countermeasures and protect against future threats.

But it's not just about the tools; it's about the skill and expertise of the analysts who wield them. Malware analysis is an art and a science, requiring a deep understanding of both the tools and the malware landscape. It's a constant game of cat and mouse, where analysts strive to stay one step ahead of cybercriminals.

So, whether you're a cybersecurity enthusiast or a seasoned professional, understanding these malware analysis tools is a crucial step in the ongoing battle against digital threats. They are the tools of the trade, the keys to unraveling the mysteries of malware, and the guardians of our digital world.

Let's delve into the world of digital forensics software and hardware, the essential tools of the trade for investigators and cybersecurity professionals. These specialized technologies are the backbone of digital investigations, enabling experts to collect, analyze, and preserve electronic evidence from a variety of devices and data sources.

First, let's talk about digital forensics software. These applications are designed to assist investigators in the retrieval and analysis of digital evidence. One of the fundamental categories of digital forensics software is imaging and acquisition tools. These tools allow investigators to create forensic copies of storage media, such as hard drives, solid-state drives, and mobile devices. They ensure that the original data remains unaltered during the investigation process, preserving its integrity for potential legal proceedings.

Imaging tools often come equipped with features for hashing, which involves generating a cryptographic hash value of the acquired data. Hashing serves as a digital fingerprint, enabling investigators to verify the integrity of the forensic image. Any changes to the data, even minor ones, would result in a different hash value, alerting investigators to potential tampering.

Once forensic images are created, analysts turn to examination and analysis tools. These software applications help investigators sift through the vast amounts of data collected during an investigation. They provide functionalities for keyword searches, file recovery, and timeline analysis. Keyword search capabilities allow investigators to pinpoint relevant information within seized data, making it easier to uncover evidence.

File recovery tools are invaluable in cases where suspects attempt to delete or hide incriminating data. These tools can often retrieve deleted files, including those from recycle bins or unallocated disk space. This capability can be critical in unearthing evidence that a suspect thought had been permanently erased.

Timeline analysis tools help investigators reconstruct the sequence of events on a digital device or within a network. They provide a chronological view of activities, such as file accesses, network connections, and system events. This timeline can be instrumental in understanding the sequence of actions taken by a suspect or in identifying anomalous behavior.

Forensic email analysis tools are another specialized category of software. These applications assist in the examination of email messages and attachments, helping investigators trace communications, identify contacts, and uncover evidence related to cybercrimes, fraud, or insider threats.

Mobile forensics tools cater to the investigation of smartphones and tablets, which have become integral to modern life. These tools support the extraction of data from mobile devices, including call logs, text messages, app data, and location information. They play a crucial role in cases involving mobile device evidence.

In addition to these software tools, digital forensics also relies on specialized hardware. Forensic hardware is used for acquiring and analyzing data from a wide range of devices, including hard drives, smartphones, GPS devices, and even embedded systems.

Write blockers are essential hardware components in the digital forensics toolkit. These devices prevent data writes to the original storage media, ensuring that investigators do not accidentally alter or corrupt evidence during the acquisition process. Write blockers come in various forms, including external devices and internal PCIe cards.

For mobile device forensics, hardware tools like cell phone extraction devices enable investigators to acquire data from smartphones and other portable devices. These tools can bypass device locks and extract data for analysis, helping uncover evidence stored on mobile devices.

Network forensic appliances are another category of hardware used to monitor and analyze network traffic. They capture and store network data for later analysis, enabling investigators to trace cyberattacks, identify malicious activity, and gather evidence related to network-based crimes.

Forensic workstations are specialized computers configured for digital forensics tasks. They are equipped with high-capacity storage, powerful processing capabilities, and multiple forensic software applications. Forensic workstations provide a controlled environment for investigators to analyze evidence without risking contamination or tampering.

In some cases, digital forensic experts employ hardware devices like logic analyzers and JTAG interfaces to interact with embedded systems, recover data from damaged devices, or perform chip-off forensics. These tools are particularly useful in situations where standard software-based approaches may not suffice.

Lastly, hardware-based encryption analysis tools help investigators decrypt and recover data from encrypted storage devices. These tools are crucial in cases where suspects have employed encryption to protect their data.

In the dynamic field of digital forensics, software and hardware tools continue to evolve to keep pace with technological advancements. New storage media, operating systems, and encryption methods present ongoing challenges for investigators. Staying updated on the latest tools and techniques is essential for those involved in digital investigations.

In summary, digital forensics software and hardware are the cornerstones of modern investigations. They enable investigators to uncover digital evidence, preserve its integrity, and analyze it to build strong cases in legal proceedings. These tools, coupled with the expertise of digital forensic professionals, play a pivotal role in maintaining the integrity of digital evidence and ensuring justice in our increasingly digital world.

Chapter 5: Static Malware Analysis Techniques

Let's dive into the fascinating world of file structure and metadata examination in the realm of digital forensics. When investigators delve into the digital landscape to uncover evidence, understanding the intricate details of files and their metadata is akin to reading the clues left at a crime scene.

First, let's unravel the concept of file structure. In the digital realm, data is organized into files and directories, forming a hierarchical structure. Think of it as a virtual filing cabinet, where documents, images, and other data are stored in folders. Each file has a unique structure that defines how its data is organized and stored. Understanding these structures is crucial for forensic analysts as they dissect the contents of storage media.

One of the fundamental aspects of file structure examination involves file system analysis. Different operating systems use various file systems to manage data storage, such as NTFS for Windows, HFS+ for macOS, and ext4 for Linux. Each file system has its own way of organizing and managing data, including how it handles file attributes, permissions, and timestamps.

File attributes, often referred to as metadata, provide valuable information about a file. Metadata includes details like the file's name, size, creation date, modification date, and access date. It's akin to the metadata embedded in a photograph, revealing when the picture was taken, its dimensions, and even the camera's make and model.

Analyzing file attributes is an essential part of digital forensics. Investigators rely on this metadata to establish timelines of events, track user activities, and identify suspicious behavior. For instance, if a suspect claims not to have accessed a specific file, examining the file's access timestamps can verify or refute their statement.

File permissions, another facet of metadata, dictate who can access, modify, or delete a file. These permissions play a critical role in digital investigations, as they help determine who had the authority to perform specific actions on a file. Unauthorized access or modifications may indicate malicious intent or misconduct.

File systems also employ data structures like file allocation tables (FAT) or master file tables (MFT) to track the physical location of file data on storage media. These structures are akin to a library catalog, guiding investigators to the precise location of data within a storage device. Examining these structures can reveal valuable insights about file relationships and data organization.

Moreover, some files contain embedded metadata known as embedded objects or embedded files. These are like hidden treasures within documents or multimedia files, such as images or videos. Embedded metadata can reveal valuable information, including authorship details, revision history, and geolocation data. It's akin to finding secret messages in the margins of a book.

Beyond examining file structures and metadata, digital forensics experts also analyze file content. This entails scrutinizing the actual data within files, such as text documents, spreadsheets, and email messages. Detecting hidden messages, encrypted data, or code snippets embedded in files requires a keen eye and specialized tools.

In addition to conventional files, forensic analysts often encounter file fragments, remnants of deleted files, and slack space, which is unused space within a file cluster. These remnants can contain valuable traces of past activities or deleted evidence. It's akin to finding hidden clues in a puzzle that has been partially disassembled.

Another critical aspect of file structure examination is identifying file relationships and dependencies. Files are not isolated entities; they often link to other files or reference external resources. Understanding these relationships is crucial for reconstructing digital events and tracking the flow of information. It's like piecing together a web of interconnected stories.

File carving is a technique used to extract files from storage media when their original file system structures are damaged or missing. Think of it as reconstructing a shattered vase from its fragments. Digital forensics experts employ file carving tools to identify and recover files based on specific file signatures or patterns.

Metadata examination extends beyond individual files and encompasses email headers, which contain valuable information about email communications.

These headers reveal details such as sender and recipient addresses, timestamps, and mail servers used in message delivery. It's akin to analyzing the postmark and address labels on physical mail.

Furthermore, analyzing metadata can extend to geospatial data embedded in files, such as GPS coordinates in photographs. This geolocation metadata can help pinpoint where an image was taken, potentially providing critical evidence in cases involving physical locations.

In the ever-evolving landscape of digital forensics, file structure and metadata examination remain core pillars of investigative techniques. By delving into file attributes, permissions, data structures, and relationships, forensic analysts uncover the hidden narratives within digital landscapes. It's a journey through the intricate details of digital data, where every file tells a story, and every piece of metadata reveals a clue.

Let's delve into the intriguing world of identifying code patterns and artifacts, a fundamental aspect of digital forensics and malware analysis. Imagine this as deciphering the unique fingerprints left by software and cybercriminals within the digital realm—a journey into the heart of the code.

First, it's essential to understand what we mean by code patterns. In the realm of digital forensics, code patterns refer to specific sequences of instructions, algorithms, or structures found in software, scripts, or malware. These patterns are akin to distinctive brushstrokes on a canvas, allowing forensic analysts to recognize the work of particular malware authors, software developers, or even hacking groups.

Identifying code patterns is a bit like being a detective in the digital world. Investigators scrutinize the code to uncover telltale signs, recurring sequences, and distinctive techniques that reveal the software's origins and purpose. It's akin to finding hidden messages in a complex puzzle, where each line of code can be a clue.

One of the key aspects of code pattern identification is recognizing the use of common libraries and frameworks. Many software applications and malware strains rely on pre-existing libraries and code snippets for efficiency and functionality. Analysts often spot these patterns by identifying code segments that match known libraries or APIs. It's akin to recognizing familiar building blocks in a city's skyline.

Moreover, code patterns extend to specific programming languages. Skilled forensic analysts can identify the unique syntax, structures, and idioms associated with particular programming languages. This skill enables them to attribute code to a specific language or development environment, narrowing down the origins of the software. It's akin to recognizing accents and dialects in spoken language.

Code obfuscation is a common technique used by malware authors to hide their code patterns. Obfuscation involves deliberately adding complexity and confusion to code to thwart analysis. Detecting and deciphering obfuscated code is like unraveling a series of locks and puzzles within a cryptic manuscript.

Another fascinating aspect of code pattern identification is identifying known algorithms or cryptographic techniques. Cybercriminals often employ encryption or hashing algorithms to protect their malicious payloads. Analysts can identify these patterns by recognizing the mathematical operations and sequences used in the code. It's akin to cracking a secret code or decoding a cipher.

Additionally, code patterns can reveal the presence of vulnerabilities or weaknesses within software. Forensic analysts often look for patterns that indicate coding errors or security flaws. These patterns can be a goldmine for cybercriminals seeking to exploit vulnerabilities. Identifying and mitigating these flaws is akin to fortifying the defenses of a digital fortress.

When dealing with malware, code patterns can uncover the malware's functionality and purpose. Analysts scrutinize the code to identify patterns related to network communication, data exfiltration, or malicious behavior. Recognizing these patterns is like deciphering the intentions of a hidden adversary.

Furthermore, code patterns extend to the analysis of file formats and document structures. Malicious documents, such as PDFs or Office files, often contain hidden code patterns or exploits. Analysts examine these file structures to identify anomalies or patterns that indicate malicious intent. It's akin to examining the blueprint of a complex device.

Code patterns also play a role in dynamic analysis. When malware is executed in a controlled environment, analysts monitor its behavior to identify patterns of suspicious or malicious activity. These patterns can include attempts to evade analysis, self-propagation, or interactions with the compromised system. Detecting these patterns is akin to observing the movements of a digital intruder.

Furthermore, code patterns can reveal the presence of rootkits or stealthy malware that attempts to hide its activities from detection. Analysts scrutinize system and memory structures to identify anomalies and patterns that indicate the presence of such stealthy software. It's akin to searching for hidden compartments in a house.

Code patterns are not limited to malicious software. They are also valuable in identifying and classifying legitimate software and applications. Analysts often create signatures or patterns for known software to differentiate it from potentially malicious code. This is akin to distinguishing between friend and foe in a crowded room.

In the dynamic field of digital forensics and malware analysis, the ability to identify code patterns and artifacts is a crucial skill. It enables investigators to trace the origins of software, uncover vulnerabilities, and detect the presence of malicious code. It's a journey through the intricacies of digital landscapes, where each line of code tells a story, and each pattern is a clue in the grand puzzle of cybersecurity.

Chapter 6: Dynamic Malware Analysis Methods

Let's delve into the captivating realm of behavioral analysis and sandbox environments, two integral components of digital forensics and cybersecurity. Imagine these as the digital watchmen, diligently observing and deciphering the behavior of software, files, and applications to uncover hidden threats and vulnerabilities.

Behavioral analysis, in the world of digital forensics and cybersecurity, is akin to being a detective who watches a suspect's every move, seeking clues to their intentions and actions. It's a technique used to understand how software or malware behaves when executed, providing insights into its functionality and potential risks.

When analysts perform behavioral analysis, they observe the interactions between software and the system on which it runs. Think of it as watching a play, where each character (the software) has its role and script (code), and the stage (the system) is set for their performance. The goal is to decipher the narrative and identify any deviations from the expected script.

One of the key aspects of behavioral analysis is monitoring system calls and API (Application Programming Interface) usage. When software runs, it makes requests to the operating system or external services through these interfaces. Analysts keep a watchful eye on these interactions, looking for any abnormal or malicious behavior. It's akin to listening in on conversations to catch suspicious dialogue.

Furthermore, behavioral analysis involves tracking file and registry system changes. When software executes, it may create, modify, or delete files and registry entries. These changes can be indicative of malware attempting to establish persistence or exfiltrate data. It's akin to examining a crime scene for signs of tampering.

Another crucial element of behavioral analysis is monitoring network communications. Malicious software often communicates with command and control servers or attempts to exfiltrate data over the network. Analysts scrutinize these network interactions to identify suspicious traffic or unauthorized data transfers. It's akin to eavesdropping on covert conversations.

Behavioral analysis also encompasses the examination of system resources and memory usage. Malware can consume excessive resources or exhibit memory manipulation techniques. Detecting these anomalies is akin to noticing a person behaving strangely at a crowded event.

Now, let's shift our focus to sandbox environments. Sandboxes are controlled, isolated spaces where software can be executed and observed without affecting the host system. Think of a sandbox as a secure laboratory where analysts can safely study potentially malicious software.

Sandbox environments mimic the functionality of a real operating system, allowing software to run as it would on a regular computer. However, the sandbox provides a controlled environment, like a laboratory with safety measures in place to prevent contamination. This isolation ensures that any malicious activity or damage caused by the software is contained within the sandbox. When analysts place suspicious software in a sandbox, they can closely monitor its behavior, interactions, and system changes. It's akin to observing a test subject in a controlled experiment, noting every action and reaction. Any malicious behavior, such as attempts to modify system files or establish unauthorized network connections, becomes apparent in the sandbox.

Moreover, sandbox environments are equipped with monitoring and logging capabilities. These logs capture detailed information about the software's actions, including system calls, file changes, network traffic, and memory usage. Analysts review these logs to gain insights into the software's behavior. It's akin to keeping a detailed journal of the test subject's activities.

Sandboxing also enables analysts to detonate potentially malicious software in a safe environment. If the software exhibits harmful behavior, it can be terminated without affecting the host system. This proactive approach is akin to testing potentially hazardous substances in a controlled laboratory setting.

In addition to behavioral analysis, sandboxes are valuable tools for dynamic malware analysis. Analysts can execute malware within the sandbox to understand its behavior, identify its capabilities, and uncover any attempts to evade detection. It's akin to dissecting a specimen to understand its anatomy and functions.

Furthermore, sandbox environments are instrumental in the development of security signatures and threat intelligence. Analysts can analyze the behavior of known malware and create signatures or patterns that can be used to detect similar threats in the future. It's akin to identifying a recurring modus operandi in criminal cases.

In the ever-evolving landscape of digital threats and cybersecurity, behavioral analysis and sandbox environments play a pivotal role in uncovering and mitigating risks. They are the watchful guardians of the digital realm, vigilant in their efforts to detect and thwart malicious software. By observing and understanding software behavior, analysts gain the upper hand in the ongoing battle against cyber threats, ensuring the security and integrity of digital systems.

Let's embark on a captivating journey into the world of dynamic code execution and behavior monitoring, two indispensable pillars of digital forensics and cybersecurity. Imagine this as a thrilling adventure through the ever-shifting landscapes of software and digital threats, where every line of code is a clue and every action a revelation.

Dynamic code execution is akin to watching a live performance, where software takes center stage and its every move is observed. When software runs in a dynamic analysis environment, it's like an actor on a stage, and forensic analysts are the attentive audience, keenly observing its behavior and interactions.

One of the primary aspects of dynamic code execution is the use of sandboxes, controlled environments that simulate the real operating system. These sandboxes provide a safe and isolated space where software can be executed without endangering the host system. It's like conducting experiments in a secure laboratory, where every variable is controlled.

Within the sandbox, software is free to perform its actions, just as a character in a play follows its script. Analysts closely monitor the software's behavior, from system calls to file accesses and network communications. It's akin to tracking the movements and dialogues of actors in a theater production, looking for deviations from the expected script.

Behavior monitoring is a critical component of dynamic code execution. Analysts keep a vigilant eye on the software's interactions with the system and network, looking for any signs of malicious or unexpected behavior. It's like being a detective at a crime scene, searching for clues and evidence of foul play.

Dynamic analysis environments also capture a wealth of data and information about the software's actions. Logs are generated, documenting every system call, file modification, and network connection. These logs become the breadcrumbs that lead analysts through the software's journey, revealing its intentions and actions. It's akin to having a detailed journal of an expedition, chronicling each step of the adventure.

Furthermore, dynamic code execution allows analysts to observe the software's memory usage and manipulation. Malware often employs memory-based techniques to hide its presence or perform malicious actions. Detecting these memory anomalies is like finding hidden compartments in a house, revealing concealed secrets.

When malware attempts to evade detection, it may employ various techniques to obfuscate its behavior. Dynamic analysis environments are equipped to handle such challenges, providing analysts with tools to uncover hidden actions and malicious intent. It's akin to deciphering a code or unraveling a puzzle within the software's behavior.

Moreover, dynamic analysis enables analysts to simulate user interactions with the software. This includes simulating mouse clicks, keyboard inputs, and interactions with the graphical user interface. It's like playing a virtual game of chess, where every move is carefully observed to anticipate the opponent's strategy.

Behavior monitoring extends to network traffic analysis within dynamic analysis environments. Analysts scrutinize the software's network interactions, looking for signs of communication with external servers or suspicious data transfers. It's akin to eavesdropping on digital conversations, listening for whispers of covert activities.

Dynamic code execution is not limited to examining the behavior of individual software. It's also valuable for analyzing the interactions between multiple software components and processes. This holistic view enables analysts to understand the intricate relationships within complex systems, much like observing the interactions between characters in a drama.

In the realm of cybersecurity, dynamic code execution is a powerful tool for dissecting malware and uncovering hidden threats. It provides a real-time view of software behavior, helping analysts identify malicious actions, data exfiltration attempts, and signs of compromise. It's a proactive approach to cybersecurity, akin to having security guards on constant patrol within the digital landscape.

Moreover, dynamic analysis environments are instrumental in the development of security signatures and threat intelligence. By observing the behavior of known malware, analysts can create patterns and signatures that aid in the detection of similar threats in the future. It's akin to recognizing recurring patterns in criminal behavior, helping law enforcement anticipate and prevent crimes.

In the ever-evolving world of digital threats and cybersecurity, dynamic code execution and behavior monitoring are the vigilant guardians of our digital landscapes. They provide a proactive defense against malware, enabling analysts to detect, analyze, and mitigate threats in real-time. It's a journey into the heart of digital systems, where every action and interaction reveals a story, and every line of code is a clue in the ongoing battle for cybersecurity.

Chapter 7: Incident Response Fundamentals

Let's embark on a fascinating journey into the world of incident identification and classification—a crucial aspect of cybersecurity and digital forensics. Imagine this as a detective's quest to uncover and categorize the various events and activities within the intricate tapestry of the digital realm.

Incident identification is like having a watchful eye over a bustling city. It involves the continuous monitoring of systems, networks, and digital landscapes to detect any anomalies or unusual activities. Think of it as being a vigilant guardian, always on the lookout for signs of trouble.

In the realm of cybersecurity, incidents can take various forms, from attempted intrusions to data breaches, malware infections, and insider threats. Identifying these incidents is akin to recognizing disturbances in the digital fabric—a sudden spike in network traffic, unauthorized access attempts, or unusual patterns of behavior.

Security tools and technologies play a pivotal role in incident identification. Intrusion detection systems (IDS), firewalls, and security information and event management (SIEM) systems are like the sentinels guarding the city gates. They analyze network traffic, log data, and system events, flagging anything that deviates from the norm.

Moreover, security analysts are the detectives of the digital world. They sift through vast amounts of data, examining logs, alerts, and system reports to identify potential incidents. It's akin to searching for clues in a vast archive of information, piecing together the narrative of a potential security event.

Incident identification extends beyond automated alerts. It involves a keen understanding of normal and abnormal behavior within an organization's digital ecosystem. Analysts develop a sense of what is typical and expected, making it easier to spot deviations or anomalies. It's akin to recognizing when something feels out of place in your own home.

Once an incident is identified, it's time to classify it—a bit like categorizing a species in the animal kingdom. Incident classification involves determining the nature and severity of the event. Is it a benign event, a potential security incident, or a full-blown cyberattack?

Classification is not a one-size-fits-all process. It depends on various factors, such as the impact on the organization, the intent behind the event, and the techniques employed by threat actors. Think of it as assigning a color to a traffic light, indicating the level of caution required.

One common classification framework is the Common Vulnerability Scoring System (CVSS). It assesses the impact and exploitability of vulnerabilities, helping analysts determine the severity of potential incidents. It's akin to assigning a threat level to a weather forecast, informing people about the potential risks.

Incident classification also considers the intent behind the event. Was it accidental, a result of misconfiguration or human error? Or was it a deliberate attempt to compromise security, an intentional act by a threat actor? It's akin to distinguishing between a friendly gesture and a suspicious action in a crowd.

Moreover, classification takes into account the techniques and tactics employed by threat actors. Did they use known malware, attempt a phishing attack, or exploit a vulnerability? Understanding the modus operandi of threat actors is like deciphering the tactics of a criminal gang.

Severity levels are assigned based on the impact an incident may have on an organization. High-severity incidents can disrupt operations, lead to data breaches, or cause financial losses. Low-severity incidents may have minimal impact and may not require immediate action. It's akin to assessing the magnitude of a natural disaster, determining the level of response needed.

Additionally, incident classification involves considering the potential for escalation. Is the incident an isolated event, or does it have the potential to evolve into a more significant security breach? This foresight is like anticipating the growth of a wildfire and taking preventive measures.

Once an incident is identified and classified, it sets the stage for incident response—an organized and coordinated effort to mitigate the threat and recover from the event. Think of it as mobilizing emergency services to address a crisis.

Incident identification and classification are the initial steps in the incident response process. They provide the foundation for understanding the nature of the threat and determining the appropriate course of action. It's akin to diagnosing a medical condition, essential for prescribing the right treatment.

In the dynamic landscape of cybersecurity, incident identification and classification are ongoing processes. Threat actors constantly evolve their tactics, and new vulnerabilities emerge. Staying vigilant and adaptable is essential for protecting digital assets and responding effectively to security incidents.

In summary, incident identification and classification are the gatekeepers of cybersecurity. They serve as the early warning system, allowing organizations to detect and categorize potential threats. By understanding the nature and severity of incidents, cybersecurity professionals can mount an effective defense and safeguard their digital domains. It's a continuous journey of vigilance and adaptability in the ever-evolving digital landscape. Let's explore the critical aspects of initial response and containment strategies in the realm of cybersecurity and incident response. Imagine this as the crucial first steps taken in the face of a digital crisis, akin to the immediate actions of a first responder at the scene of an emergency.

When an incident is identified and classified, the clock starts ticking, much like the first moments after a fire alarm sounds. The initial response is all about swift and decisive action, a coordinated effort to assess the situation and take steps to mitigate the threat.

One of the primary objectives of the initial response is to contain the incident—similar to isolating a contagious patient to prevent the spread of disease. Containment involves limiting the impact of the incident and preventing it from escalating further. It's like creating a barrier to contain a chemical spill.

Containment strategies vary depending on the nature of the incident. For example, in the case of a malware infection, isolating the affected system from the network is a common containment measure. It's akin to quarantining a sick individual to prevent the infection from spreading.

Moreover, containment may involve disabling compromised accounts or services, closing vulnerabilities, or blocking malicious network traffic. It's like shutting off a leaky faucet to stop the flow of water, preventing further damage.

In addition to technical measures, containment often requires communication and coordination among various teams within an organization. It's akin to orchestrating a response effort, where everyone has a role to play in containing the incident and preventing its spread.

While containment is critical, it's not the only focus of the initial response. Another essential aspect is preserving evidence—much like securing a crime scene to ensure that valuable clues are not tampered with or lost. Preserving evidence is crucial for later analysis and investigation.

Preservation involves taking snapshots of affected systems, capturing log data, and preserving memory dumps. It's akin to collecting samples and photographs at a crime scene, ensuring that nothing is disturbed or altered.

Furthermore, the initial response includes notifying relevant stakeholders and authorities. This may involve alerting law enforcement, regulatory bodies, or affected parties, such as customers or partners. It's akin to reporting an incident to emergency services, ensuring that the right authorities are informed.

Moreover, the initial response often necessitates the involvement of incident response teams and experts. These teams are like the specialized units that arrive at the scene of a crisis, bringing their expertise and tools to bear on the situation. Incident responders work to assess the scope and impact of the incident, identify the root cause, and develop a plan for containment and recovery.

The containment strategy may also involve creating a virtual clean room—a controlled environment where affected systems can be analyzed and repaired without risking further contamination. Think of it as a sterile operating room where a surgeon can perform a delicate procedure.

Additionally, initial response efforts should include ongoing monitoring and validation. It's not enough to contain the incident; organizations must ensure that the threat is effectively neutralized. Continuous monitoring helps detect any resurgence or lingering traces of the threat. It's akin to checking a patient's vital signs even after a successful surgery.

Furthermore, initial response and containment strategies should consider the potential for legal and regulatory implications. Incident responders must be mindful of privacy laws, data breach notification requirements, and other legal obligations. It's akin to following the law and regulations while managing a public crisis.

Moreover, organizations often develop incident response playbooks—a set of predefined procedures and guidelines for responding to specific types of incidents. These playbooks are like emergency response manuals, providing step-by-step instructions for containment and recovery. They ensure that response efforts are organized and efficient.

In the dynamic world of cybersecurity, initial response and containment are pivotal moments in the incident response process. They set the stage for subsequent actions, from recovery and remediation to analysis and post-incident review. A well-executed initial response can mitigate the impact of an incident, minimize damage, and ultimately safeguard an organization's digital assets.

In summary, initial response and containment strategies are the first steps in managing cybersecurity incidents. They involve swift action, effective coordination, and decisive measures to limit the impact of threats. Like first responders in an emergency, incident responders play a critical role in protecting digital domains and ensuring a swift return to normalcy after an incident.

Chapter 8: Network Forensics and Malware

Let's dive into the captivating world of network traffic analysis techniques, a fundamental aspect of cybersecurity that's akin to exploring the intricate highways and byways of the digital realm. Imagine this as a journey through the bustling streets of the internet, where every packet of data carries a story, and every connection is a potential clue.

Network traffic analysis is the art of examining the data that flows through a network—much like watching the traffic on a busy city street. It's a bit like being a traffic cop, monitoring the vehicles (data packets) as they move, and ensuring that everything is in order.

One of the primary goals of network traffic analysis is to detect abnormal or suspicious activity within the network. Think of it as spotting erratic driving behavior on the road—a sudden lane change or excessive speed. In the digital world, these anomalies may indicate security threats, such as malware infections or unauthorized access attempts.

To achieve this, network traffic analysis tools and technologies continuously capture and scrutinize network packets—those tiny units of data that travel between devices on a network. It's akin to intercepting and inspecting every vehicle passing through a toll booth.

Moreover, network traffic analysis involves monitoring and logging various aspects of network communications. This includes tracking the source and destination of data packets, the protocols used, and the timing of communications. Think of it as noting the license plates, routes, and schedules of vehicles on the road.

One critical aspect of network traffic analysis is identifying patterns and trends. Analysts look for recurring behaviors or anomalies that may indicate security incidents. It's like noticing that certain vehicles always take a particular route or that a driver consistently speeds through a stop sign.

Another essential task is monitoring for known attack signatures. Security professionals maintain databases of known attack patterns and behaviors. When network traffic analysis tools detect these signatures, it's akin to recognizing the tactics used by a known criminal. This recognition triggers alerts and responses.

Furthermore, network traffic analysis techniques include deep packet inspection (DPI), which involves examining the contents of network packets. DPI is like opening the trunk of a vehicle to inspect its cargo. It allows analysts to uncover hidden threats or malware payloads within network traffic.

Additionally, behavioral analysis plays a crucial role in network traffic analysis. This approach involves creating baselines of normal network behavior and flagging deviations from those baselines. Think of it as recognizing when a car behaves unusually on the road, such as erratic swerving or sudden stops.

Moreover, network traffic analysis is not limited to internal network monitoring. It extends to monitoring external communications as well. Organizations often use intrusion detection and prevention systems (IDS/IPS) to scrutinize incoming and outgoing network traffic for signs of malicious activity. It's akin to inspecting vehicles entering and leaving a secure compound.

Intrusion detection systems are like vigilant guards at the gates of a fortress. They analyze network traffic in real-time, looking for signs of unauthorized access or suspicious behavior. When they detect anomalies, it's akin to spotting an intruder attempting to breach the defenses.

Additionally, network traffic analysis techniques extend to monitoring for distributed denial of service (DDoS) attacks. These attacks flood a network with traffic to overwhelm its resources. Network traffic analysis tools can identify unusual spikes in traffic and mitigate DDoS attacks by diverting or blocking malicious traffic. Think of it as managing traffic flow during a parade to prevent gridlock.

Moreover, network traffic analysis tools often provide visualization capabilities, creating graphical representations of network traffic patterns. These visualizations are like traffic maps, allowing analysts to see the flow of data and detect anomalies more easily. It's akin to having a bird's-eye view of the city's streets.

Network traffic analysis techniques are not limited to identifying threats; they also play a role in network performance monitoring. By analyzing network traffic, organizations can optimize their networks, identify bottlenecks, and ensure efficient data transfer. It's akin to managing traffic flow to reduce congestion on busy streets.

Furthermore, network traffic analysis techniques are essential for incident response. When a security incident occurs, analysts can use network traffic data to reconstruct the timeline of events, trace the source of the attack, and understand its impact. Think of it as reviewing surveillance footage to piece together a crime.

In the dynamic world of cybersecurity, network traffic analysis is a critical tool for identifying and mitigating threats. It's like having vigilant traffic cops patrolling the digital highways, ensuring that data flows smoothly and securely. By analyzing network traffic, organizations can safeguard their digital assets and protect against a wide range of cyber threats.

Let's embark on a fascinating exploration of two essential topics in the realm of cybersecurity: malware propagation and command and control (C2) analysis. Think of this journey as a quest to understand how malicious software spreads and how it communicates with its masters, much like unraveling the secrets of a covert operation.

Malware propagation is the process by which malicious software spreads from one system to another. It's like the way a contagious illness can pass from person to person. Malware has its methods, often exploiting vulnerabilities in software or tricking users into running it.

One common method of propagation is through email attachments or links. When users unknowingly open an infected attachment or click a malicious link, it's akin to allowing a virus to enter their system. The malware then seeks to replicate and spread further, much like a virus replicates within a host.

Another avenue for malware propagation is through infected removable media, such as USB drives. When a user inserts an infected USB drive into their computer, it's akin to introducing a Trojan horse into their digital fortress. The malware can then infiltrate and begin its mission.

Moreover, some malware can exploit vulnerabilities in network services or operating systems. It's like finding a weak point in a fortress's defenses and sneaking in through the cracks. Once inside, the malware can propagate to other vulnerable systems within the network.

Malware authors are quite cunning. They often use social engineering techniques to trick users into running malicious code. For example, a phishing email that appears to be from a trusted source may prompt the user to open an attachment or click a link, inadvertently introducing malware into their system. It's akin to a con artist deceiving someone into making a regrettable decision.

Now, let's shift our focus to command and control analysis, a critical aspect of cybersecurity. Command and control (C2) servers are like the puppet masters pulling the strings of malware-infected systems. These servers issue instructions to the malware and receive stolen data in return.

C2 analysis involves uncovering the communication channels between infected systems and C2 servers. Think of it as intercepting covert messages between spies and their handlers. Understanding these communication channels is essential for mitigating the threat and neutralizing the malware's capabilities.

One common method used by C2 servers is domain generation algorithms (DGAs). These algorithms generate a large number of domain names that the malware can use to communicate with the C2 server. It's akin to spies using coded messages that change regularly to avoid detection.

C2 analysis also involves monitoring network traffic for signs of suspicious or unauthorized communications. Analysts look for patterns and anomalies in the data flow, much like detectives scrutinize phone records for unusual calls. Any unexpected network traffic can be a clue that the malware is attempting to establish contact with its C2 server.

Furthermore, analyzing the behavior of malware-infected systems can reveal clues about C2 communications. When malware runs on a system, it may exhibit specific behaviors, such as making unusual network connections or sending data to unknown destinations. It's akin to noticing a person acting strangely and investigating the reason behind their behavior.

In addition, examining malware code can provide insights into its C2 capabilities. Analysts dissect the code to identify how it communicates with the C2 server and what data it sends and receives. It's akin to decoding secret messages to understand the intentions of an adversary.

C2 analysis extends to tracking the infrastructure used by attackers, including the hosting providers and IP addresses associated with C2 servers. By identifying and blocking these malicious infrastructure elements, organizations can disrupt the malware's ability to communicate with its controllers. Think of it as shutting down a criminal hideout to prevent further criminal activities.

Moreover, threat intelligence plays a significant role in C2 analysis. Security professionals collect and share information about known C2 servers, malware families, and attack techniques. This intelligence helps organizations detect and respond to C2 communications more effectively. It's akin to law enforcement agencies sharing information about criminal organizations to coordinate efforts and combat crime.

Command and control analysis also involves understanding the goals and objectives of the threat actors behind the malware. By uncovering their motivations, organizations can develop strategies to thwart their activities. It's akin to profiling criminals to predict their next moves and prevent future crimes.

In the ever-evolving landscape of cybersecurity, malware propagation and command and control analysis are essential components of defense. By understanding how malware spreads and communicates, organizations can detect and respond to threats more effectively. It's like staying one step ahead of spies and saboteurs in the digital age, ensuring the security and integrity of digital systems.

Chapter 9: Rootkits and Persistence Mechanisms

Let's dive into the intriguing world of rootkit architecture. It's like exploring the hidden passages and secret chambers of a digital fortress, where malicious software lurks in the shadows, undetected by the average user.

At its core, a rootkit is a type of malicious software designed to gain unauthorized access to a computer or system while remaining hidden from detection. Think of it as a digital ninja that silently infiltrates a system, often with the highest level of privileges, known as "root" or "administrator" access.

Now, the architecture of a rootkit is a sophisticated and cunning design. It's like the blueprint for a covert operation, with multiple layers of functionality to ensure stealth and persistence.

The first layer of a rootkit is the user mode component. This component operates in the same memory space as normal user-level applications, making it difficult to detect. It's like an undercover operative blending into a crowd, unnoticed by casual observers.

The user mode component often has a benign-sounding name, making it less suspicious. For example, it may masquerade as a legitimate system process or application. It's akin to a spy using a false identity to move freely in enemy territory.

Beyond the user mode, a rootkit may also employ a kernel mode component. This component operates at the core of the operating system, giving it extensive control and access. Think of it as the mastermind behind the scenes, pulling the strings without anyone noticing.

The kernel mode component can intercept and manipulate system calls, which are requests made by applications to the operating system. It's like a puppeteer controlling marionettes, directing the actions of the system while remaining hidden.

To maintain persistence, rootkits often employ various techniques. One common method is to modify the Master Boot Record (MBR) or the boot loader of the operating system. It's akin to changing the locks on all the doors of a building to ensure continued access.

Another persistence technique involves adding entries in the system's startup configuration, ensuring that the rootkit is loaded every time the computer boots. This is like embedding a spy in the inner circle of an organization, allowing them to influence decisions from within.

Moreover, rootkits can manipulate system drivers, replacing legitimate drivers with malicious ones. It's akin to infiltrating a trusted group with a double agent, who can subtly sabotage operations.

Rootkit architecture often includes stealth mechanisms to evade detection. This may involve hooking system functions, intercepting and modifying data as it flows between the operating system and applications. It's like intercepting letters in the mail and altering their contents before delivery.

Some rootkits employ anti-debugging and anti-forensics techniques to make it difficult for security analysts to investigate their activities. These techniques can include monitoring for debugging tools and tampering with log files. It's akin to leaving false clues at a crime scene to mislead investigators.

Furthermore, rootkits may use encryption and obfuscation to conceal their code and communications. This is like encoding messages in a secret language that only the intended recipients can understand.

In addition to stealth and persistence, rootkits often have backdoor functionality. This allows threat actors to remotely control the infected system, much like having a hidden entrance to a secure building that only authorized individuals can use.

The communication between the rootkit and the external command and control server is often encrypted and designed to blend in with legitimate network traffic. It's like spies using coded messages to communicate with their handlers without raising suspicion.

Rootkit architecture can also involve the ability to download and execute additional malicious payloads, expanding the capabilities of the malware. Think of it as giving a spy access to a cache of weapons and tools to carry out their mission.

Now, detecting and removing rootkits is no easy task. Security professionals employ specialized tools and techniques to uncover these hidden threats. It's like sending in a crack team of investigators with the skills and tools to root out espionage.

Rootkit analysis often involves memory forensics, examining the system's memory to identify anomalies and signs of rootkit activity. It's akin to searching for hidden compartments or secret passages within a building.

Additionally, security experts use rootkit scanners and anti-rootkit software to detect and remove these stealthy intruders. Think of these tools as the digital equivalent of bug detectors used to uncover hidden surveillance devices.

Understanding rootkit architecture is essential for cybersecurity professionals. It helps them recognize the tactics and techniques employed by these covert threats, enabling them to develop strategies for detection and mitigation.

In the ongoing battle against cyber threats, rootkits are formidable adversaries. However, with knowledge and vigilance, security experts can uncover their hidden operations and protect digital systems from infiltration and compromise. It's like shining a light into the darkest corners to reveal the hidden dangers lurking within.

Chapter 10: Real-World Case Studies in Cybersecurity

Let's embark on a fascinating journey into the world of detecting and mitigating persistent threats in the realm of cybersecurity. Think of this as an adventure where we uncover the hidden dangers that linger within digital landscapes and explore strategies to ward off these tenacious adversaries.

Persistent threats, my dear reader, are like digital ghosts that refuse to disappear. They are sophisticated and determined, often targeting high-value assets within an organization. Detecting and mitigating these threats require a combination of technology, expertise, and vigilance.

To begin our journey, let's understand what makes a threat persistent. Persistent threats are not your run-of-the-mill cyberattacks; they are designed to remain undetected for extended periods. It's like an expert jewel thief who meticulously plans every detail to evade capture.

These threats often involve advanced malware and tactics, such as rootkits, that can hide within a system for months or even years. They operate stealthily, much like a skilled spy operating undercover within an organization.

Now, the journey of detecting persistent threats begins with comprehensive network monitoring and analysis. Think of it as setting up surveillance cameras throughout a city to catch a criminal on the move. In the digital world, this means collecting and analyzing vast amounts of data to identify abnormal patterns and behaviors.

One key technique used in detecting persistent threats is anomaly detection. It's like having an alert system that triggers when something unusual happens. In cybersecurity, anomaly detection algorithms analyze network traffic and system activity to identify deviations from normal behavior, potentially signaling the presence of a persistent threat.

Moreover, security information and event management (SIEM) solutions play a pivotal role in the detection process. These systems aggregate and correlate data from various sources, such as network logs, endpoint devices, and security appliances. Think of them as central command centers where all incoming information is analyzed for signs of trouble.

Additionally, threat intelligence feeds provide valuable insights into known threat actors, attack techniques, and indicators of compromise. It's akin to having a network of informants who share information about criminal activities. These feeds help organizations proactively identify and respond to persistent threats.

In the quest to detect persistent threats, security professionals also conduct endpoint monitoring. This involves examining the activities of individual devices within an organization's network. It's like having investigators shadow a suspect to gather evidence. By closely monitoring endpoints, security teams can identify suspicious activities or unauthorized access.

Furthermore, sandboxing is a crucial tool in the arsenal against persistent threats. Sandboxes are controlled environments where potentially malicious files or programs can be executed safely for analysis. It's akin to studying a dangerous specimen under a microscope while keeping it contained. Sandboxing helps security experts understand the behavior of suspicious code without risking an infection.

Now, once a persistent threat is detected, the next phase of our journey begins—mitigation. Mitigating a persistent threat is like setting a trap to catch a cunning adversary. It involves isolating the threat, removing it, and fortifying defenses to prevent future incursions.

One common mitigation strategy is isolating compromised systems. Think of it as quarantining a contagious patient to prevent the spread of disease. Isolating compromised systems involves disconnecting them from the network to prevent the threat from moving laterally within the organization.

Additionally, security teams often employ incident response playbooks. These playbooks are like well-thought-out battle plans that outline step-by-step actions to contain and mitigate a threat. They ensure that responses are coordinated and efficient, like a well-executed military operation.

Moreover, root cause analysis is a critical aspect of mitigation. It's like dissecting a puzzle to understand how all the pieces fit together. Security professionals investigate how the persistent threat gained access and what vulnerabilities it exploited. This knowledge helps organizations patch vulnerabilities and strengthen their defenses.

Furthermore, forensic analysis plays a role in understanding the extent of the damage caused by a persistent threat. Think of it as gathering evidence at a crime scene to build a case against a criminal. Forensic experts examine affected systems, collect digital artifacts, and reconstruct the timeline of the attack.

In the battle against persistent threats, organizations often engage in threat hunting. Threat hunting is like actively searching for hidden adversaries within an organization's network. Security teams proactively seek out signs of suspicious activity, anomalies, or indicators of compromise that might have gone unnoticed.

Moreover, organizations may employ deception techniques as part of their mitigation strategy. These techniques involve creating decoy systems and data to lure attackers into revealing themselves. It's akin to setting traps to catch burglars in the act.

Additionally, threat intelligence continues to play a crucial role in mitigation. Security experts continuously update their knowledge of emerging threats and attack techniques. It's like staying informed about the latest criminal trends to anticipate and counteract the actions of persistent adversaries.

The journey of detecting and mitigating persistent threats is ongoing and ever-evolving. Cybersecurity professionals must remain vigilant, adapt to new tactics employed by persistent threats, and continuously improve their defenses. It's like a perpetual game of cat and mouse, where defenders strive to stay one step ahead of their digital adversaries.

In summary, detecting and mitigating persistent threats is a complex and dynamic process that requires a combination of technology, expertise, and determination. By employing advanced detection techniques and proactive mitigation strategies, organizations can safeguard their digital assets and protect themselves against persistent adversaries.

Let's embark on a journey through the annals of cybersecurity history, where we'll explore some of the most notable breaches and unravel the lessons they teach us about the ever-evolving landscape of digital security. Think of this as a captivating detective story, where we uncover the motives, methods, and consequences of these cyber-attacks.

Our journey begins with the Target breach of 2013, a watershed moment in cybersecurity. Imagine this breach as a heist in a bustling shopping mall, where cybercriminals infiltrated Target's payment system, compromising credit card data of millions of customers. This breach highlighted the vulnerability of large retailers to sophisticated attacks and underscored the need for robust security measures.

Moving forward, we encounter the Equifax breach of 2017, a stark reminder of the consequences of inadequate cybersecurity. In this breach, personal and financial information of nearly 147 million individuals was exposed. It's like a treasure trove of sensitive data falling into the wrong hands. The Equifax breach emphasized the critical importance of patching known vulnerabilities promptly and implementing strong access controls.

Now, let's delve into the Yahoo breaches of 2013 and 2014, which had far-reaching implications. Imagine this as a digital espionage saga, where state-sponsored hackers gained access to over a billion Yahoo accounts, compromising email communications and personal information. These breaches shed light on the increasing sophistication of nation-state actors and the importance of user security awareness.

In the realm of social media, the Facebook-Cambridge Analytica scandal of 2018 brought privacy concerns into the spotlight. It's like a breach of trust among friends, where user data was harvested without consent for political purposes. This incident emphasized the need for transparency in data collection practices and user control over personal information.

Moving into the healthcare sector, the Anthem breach of 2015 exposed sensitive medical and personal records of nearly 80 million individuals. Think of it as a breach of doctor-patient confidentiality on a massive scale. The Anthem breach underscored the importance of safeguarding healthcare data and complying with industry-specific regulations.

Cybersecurity breaches also have a political dimension, as exemplified by the Democratic National Committee (DNC) breach of 2016. This breach, attributed to state-sponsored hackers, involved the theft and release of sensitive political emails. It's like a digital espionage operation with political ramifications, highlighting the need for robust email security and threat intelligence.

In the financial sector, the Bangladesh Bank heist of 2016 was a daring cyber-attack that resulted in the theft of $81 million. Imagine this as a digital bank robbery orchestrated by hackers who infiltrated the bank's systems and attempted to transfer funds to fake accounts. The Bangladesh Bank breach emphasized the importance of secure financial transactions and robust authentication mechanisms.

The Marriott International breach of 2018 exposed the personal information of approximately 500 million guests. It's like a breach of trust in the hospitality industry, where sensitive data, including passport numbers, was compromised. This breach highlighted the need for rigorous third-party vendor assessments and data encryption practices.

Now, let's shift our focus to the devastating NotPetya ransomware attack of 2017, which caused widespread disruption and financial losses. Think of this as a digital contagion that spread rapidly, infecting organizations worldwide. NotPetya showcased the destructive capabilities of ransomware and the importance of regularly updating and patching systems.

The SolarWinds supply chain attack of 2020 was a sophisticated operation that compromised software updates, allowing threat actors to infiltrate numerous organizations. It's like a Trojan horse that sneaked into the heart of critical infrastructure. The SolarWinds breach emphasized the need for secure software supply chains and continuous monitoring for unusual network activity.

Additionally, the Colonial Pipeline ransomware attack of 2021 had a direct impact on critical infrastructure, causing fuel shortages in parts of the United States. Imagine this as a cyber-attack with real-world consequences, disrupting fuel supply chains and highlighting the vulnerability of essential services to digital threats. The Colonial Pipeline incident underscored the importance of securing critical infrastructure against cyber threats.

As we reflect on these notable breaches, several key lessons emerge. First and foremost, the cybersecurity landscape is constantly evolving, with threat actors becoming increasingly sophisticated. Organizations must adapt and invest in robust security measures to defend against these evolving threats.

Moreover, breaches often result from a combination of technical vulnerabilities and human errors. Therefore, cybersecurity awareness and training for employees are crucial components of defense. It's like teaching everyone in a city to lock their doors and be vigilant against potential intruders.

Additionally, timely detection and response are essential. Organizations need to invest in advanced threat detection technologies and incident response plans to minimize the impact of breaches when they occur. Think of this as having a rapid-response team ready to mitigate the effects of a disaster.

Furthermore, breaches have legal and regulatory implications, underscoring the importance of compliance with data protection laws and industry-specific regulations. It's like obeying traffic rules to avoid accidents and penalties.

In summary, the world of cybersecurity is filled with challenges and risks, but it's also a realm of constant innovation and adaptation. By learning from the lessons of notable breaches and implementing robust security practices, organizations can better protect themselves in this digital age. It's like fortifying the defenses of a digital fortress, ensuring that it stands strong against the ever-present threats in the cyber landscape.

BOOK 2
MALWARE DETECTION AND ANALYSIS IN CYBERSECURIT
A PRACTICAL APPROACH

ROB BOTWRIGHT

Chapter 1: Introduction to Malware Detection

Let's embark on a journey to explore the significance of malware detection in the intricate world of cybersecurity. Think of this as a quest to understand the guardians that stand watch over our digital realms, protecting us from insidious threats that lurk in the shadows.

Malware, my dear reader, is like a digital plague. It encompasses a wide array of malicious software designed to infiltrate, disrupt, or compromise computer systems. From viruses and worms to Trojans and ransomware, malware comes in many forms, each with its own sinister intent.

The significance of malware detection lies in its role as a vigilant sentry. Imagine it as the watchful guardian of a castle, scanning the horizon for any signs of approaching danger. In the digital realm, malware detection is the first line of defense against cyber threats.

Detection begins with the watchful eyes of antivirus programs. These digital guardians scan files and applications for known malware signatures. It's like having a team of sentinels at the gates, checking every visitor against a list of known troublemakers.

But the world of malware is crafty and ever-changing. Threat actors continuously evolve their tactics, creating new strains of malware that elude traditional detection methods. This is where heuristic analysis comes into play. It's like training the guards to recognize suspicious behavior, even if they haven't seen the intruder's face before. Heuristic analysis identifies malware based on behavioral patterns, helping detect previously unseen threats.

Furthermore, signature-based detection and heuristic analysis are complemented by machine learning algorithms. These digital sentinels are like well-trained hounds, learning from past encounters to recognize new threats. Machine learning algorithms analyze vast datasets to identify anomalies and patterns associated with malware.

Intrusion detection systems (IDS) play a pivotal role in network security. Think of them as the guardians of the castle's walls, constantly monitoring network traffic for unusual activity. IDS can detect signs of a malware infection, such as suspicious network connections or unauthorized access attempts.

Beyond the realm of traditional antivirus programs and heuristic analysis, there are advanced threat detection solutions. These sentinels are like elite intelligence agents, using behavioral analytics, threat intelligence feeds, and sandboxing to uncover even the most sophisticated threats.

Behavioral analytics monitors user and system behavior for deviations from the norm. It's akin to having a detective who studies people's habits to identify potential criminals. Behavioral analytics can detect unusual patterns of activity that may indicate a malware infection or a cyber-attack in progress.

Threat intelligence feeds provide real-time information about emerging threats and attack techniques. Think of them as intelligence briefings that keep the sentinels informed about the latest enemy tactics. Armed with this knowledge, security teams can proactively defend against new and evolving threats.

Sandboxing, on the other hand, is like a controlled environment where suspicious files and programs are executed to observe their behavior. It's akin to testing a potentially dangerous substance in a secure laboratory. Sandboxing helps security professionals understand how a file or program interacts with the system, allowing them to identify and isolate malware.

But detection is only the first step. Once malware is detected, it must be dealt with swiftly. Think of it as apprehending a criminal who has breached the castle's defenses. Incident response teams swing into action, isolating infected systems, removing malware, and mitigating the damage.

Furthermore, malware detection is not limited to the realm of traditional computers. Mobile devices, IoT devices, and even industrial control systems are vulnerable to malware attacks. These digital sentinels protect not only our laptops and desktops but also the vast array of connected devices that permeate our lives.

The significance of malware detection extends to safeguarding sensitive data. In an age where personal and financial information is stored digitally, malware detection is the gatekeeper that ensures our data remains secure. Think of it as a guardian of your most precious possessions, standing watch to prevent theft and compromise.

Moreover, the consequences of malware attacks can be devastating. Ransomware, for example, can encrypt critical data, rendering it inaccessible until a ransom is paid. It's like having an intruder lock all your valuables in a secure vault and demand a hefty ransom for the key. Malware detection helps prevent such scenarios by identifying and neutralizing ransomware before it can do harm.

Malware detection is also essential for safeguarding critical infrastructure. Think of it as a guardian of power grids, water treatment plants, and transportation systems. A malware infection in these systems can have far-reaching consequences, affecting the lives of countless individuals. The significance of malware detection in critical infrastructure cannot be overstated.

Additionally, malware detection is a vital component of compliance with data protection regulations. Organizations must demonstrate that they have implemented robust security measures to safeguard sensitive data. Think of it as obeying traffic rules to avoid accidents and penalties. Malware detection is one of the key measures that ensure compliance with these regulations.

In summary, the significance of malware detection in the realm of cybersecurity is paramount. It's the guardian that stands watch over our digital domains, protecting us from an array of threats. From traditional antivirus programs to advanced threat detection solutions, these sentinels work tirelessly to keep our systems and data safe. In an ever-evolving landscape of cyber threats, malware detection remains our steadfast protector, ensuring that we can navigate the digital world with confidence and security.

Let's dive into the intricate world of malware detection, where we'll explore the various approaches and the unique challenges that cybersecurity experts face in this ongoing battle against digital threats. Think of this as a journey into the heart of the digital battlefield, where defenders and adversaries engage in a constant game of cat and mouse.

To begin our exploration, let's first understand that malware detection is like a digital detective's work. It involves identifying and neutralizing malicious software that seeks to infiltrate and compromise our digital lives. Just as a detective uses clues and evidence to solve a case, cybersecurity experts employ various methods to detect and combat malware.

One of the fundamental approaches to malware detection is signature-based detection. Think of this as recognizing a criminal by their fingerprints. Signature-based detection involves comparing files and programs to a database of known malware signatures. If there's a match, it's a red flag, indicating the presence of malware. However, this approach has limitations, as it can only detect known threats, leaving new and evolving malware undetected.

Heuristic analysis comes into play as a complementary approach. It's like teaching the detective to recognize suspicious behavior, even if they've never seen a particular criminal before. Heuristic analysis identifies malware based on behavioral patterns and anomalies.

This method is effective in detecting previously unseen threats but may also generate false positives.

Machine learning, another essential tool in the arsenal of malware detection, is like having a detective with a photographic memory. Machine learning algorithms analyze vast amounts of data to recognize patterns and anomalies associated with malware. This approach allows for the detection of both known and novel threats, making it a powerful ally in the fight against malware.

Behavioral analytics is a proactive method that monitors user and system behavior for deviations from the norm. Imagine it as having a detective who knows the habits of everyone in a neighborhood and can spot unusual activities. Behavioral analytics can detect suspicious patterns that may indicate a malware infection or a cyber-attack in progress.

Furthermore, intrusion detection systems (IDS) act as vigilant sentinels guarding the castle walls. These systems continuously monitor network traffic for unusual activity, much like guards scanning the horizon for signs of approaching danger. IDS can detect signs of a malware infection, such as suspicious network connections or unauthorized access attempts.

Threat intelligence feeds, on the other hand, are like intelligence briefings for the detective. They provide real-time information about emerging threats and attack techniques. Armed with this knowledge, security teams can proactively defend against new and evolving malware threats.

Sandboxing is a controlled environment where suspicious files and programs are executed to observe their behavior. Think of it as testing a potentially dangerous substance in a secure laboratory. Sandboxing helps security professionals understand how a file or program interacts with the system, allowing them to identify and isolate malware.

Now, let's delve into the unique challenges that malware detection faces. The digital landscape is a constantly shifting battlefield, with threat actors becoming increasingly sophisticated. Malware is evolving rapidly, employing evasion techniques and polymorphic code that change its appearance, making it difficult to detect using traditional methods.

Moreover, there's the challenge of zero-day vulnerabilities. These are like undiscovered traps in the castle's defenses, waiting for an attacker to exploit them. Zero-day vulnerabilities are unknown to the vendor and, therefore, lack patches or signatures for detection. Detecting and mitigating threats that exploit zero-day vulnerabilities require advanced heuristic and behavioral analysis.

Another challenge is the sheer volume of malware samples generated daily. It's like a detective sifting through an ever-expanding pile of case files. Automated malware analysis tools are essential to process and categorize these samples efficiently. However, this volume can overwhelm traditional detection methods, necessitating the use of machine learning and artificial intelligence.

Furthermore, malware authors often employ obfuscation techniques to hide their creations. It's like criminals wearing disguises to avoid detection. Malware can be encrypted, packed, or manipulated to evade signature-based detection. Detecting obfuscated malware requires advanced analysis techniques and constant adaptation.

The rise of fileless malware poses yet another challenge. This type of malware operates in memory, leaving no trace on disk for traditional antivirus programs to detect. It's like a criminal who erases all fingerprints from the crime scene. Detecting fileless malware requires monitoring system memory and behavior, making it a complex task.

Additionally, there's the challenge of false positives. These are like innocent people mistakenly identified as criminals. Heuristic and behavioral analysis, while powerful, may sometimes flag legitimate software as malicious due to unusual behavior. Balancing detection accuracy with minimizing false positives is a delicate task for cybersecurity experts.

Lastly, malware often operates as part of a larger attack campaign. It's like a detective unraveling a complex criminal conspiracy. Detecting and mitigating malware in the context of a sophisticated attack requires comprehensive threat intelligence and analysis.

In summary, the approaches and challenges of malware detection paint a complex and dynamic picture of the cybersecurity landscape. Detecting malware requires a multifaceted approach that combines signature-based detection, heuristic analysis, machine learning, behavioral analytics, and more. However, as malware evolves and threats become more sophisticated, cybersecurity experts must continually adapt their strategies and tools to stay one step ahead of their digital adversaries. This ongoing battle in the digital realm underscores the importance of robust malware detection methods and the need for constant vigilance in the face of ever-evolving threats.

Chapter 2: Malware Taxonomy and Characteristics

Let's embark on a fascinating journey into the realm of malware classification, where we'll unravel the intricate world of malicious software and understand how experts classify these digital adversaries. Think of this as an exploration of the many faces of cyber threats, where each type and family of malware has its distinct characteristics and purposes.

Malware, my dear reader, is like a digital underworld populated by various criminals with unique modi operandi. To navigate this world, we need a classification system, much like the way we categorize different species in the animal kingdom. This system helps cybersecurity experts understand, analyze, and combat malware effectively.

First and foremost, we have viruses. These digital villains are like the common cold of the cyber world. Viruses attach themselves to legitimate files and programs, replicating and spreading when the infected files are executed. They can cause a wide range of issues, from data corruption to system crashes. The classification of viruses is based on their behavior, infection methods, and payloads.

Next up, we have worms, which are akin to digital parasites. Worms are self-replicating programs that don't need a host file to propagate. They spread through network vulnerabilities, infecting other computers within the same network. Worms can create botnets and launch large-scale attacks. Their classification often revolves around their propagation methods and payloads.

Trojans, on the other hand, are like digital infiltrators wearing disguises. These malicious programs masquerade as legitimate software, tricking users into installing them. Once inside a system, Trojans can perform a variety of actions, from stealing sensitive data to facilitating remote access for attackers. Classifying Trojans depends on their intended purpose and functionality.

Ransomware is a particularly menacing type of malware, reminiscent of digital kidnappers. Ransomware encrypts a victim's files or entire system, demanding a ransom for the decryption key. This type of malware has gained notoriety for its ability to disrupt businesses and extort money from individuals. Ransomware classification often focuses on the encryption methods and ransom notes used.

Spyware operates covertly, much like digital spies. These programs gather information about a user's online activities, such as keystrokes, website visits, and login credentials. Spyware can be used for surveillance, espionage, or identity theft. Classifying spyware depends on its data collection methods and the level of intrusiveness.

Adware, while less malicious, is like a persistent salesman in the digital world. It displays unwanted advertisements to users, often in the form of pop-ups or banners. Adware can be annoying and may slow down system performance. Classifying adware involves identifying its delivery methods and the extent of user disruption.

Rootkits are like digital moles, burrowing deep into a system's core. These malicious programs hide themselves and other malware from detection, making them challenging to remove. Rootkits often accompany other types of malware and are classified based on their root-level access and stealth techniques.

Botnets are like digital armies under the control of a single commander. These networks of compromised computers, known as zombies or bots, can be used for various purposes, including launching distributed denial-of-service (DDoS) attacks, sending spam, or stealing data. Botnet classification revolves around their command and control infrastructure and the activities they engage in.

Backdoors are like hidden trapdoors in the digital fortress. These unauthorized access points allow attackers to bypass security measures and gain control over a system. Backdoors can be used for remote control, data theft, or launching further attacks. Classifying backdoors depends on their methods of entry and the privileges they grant.

Keyloggers are like digital eavesdroppers, recording every keystroke made by a user. These malicious programs capture sensitive information, such as passwords and credit card numbers. Keyloggers can be used for identity theft or gaining unauthorized access. Their classification centers on their logging methods and data exfiltration techniques.

Now, you might wonder, "How do experts classify these various types of malware into families?" Well, it's a bit like grouping animals based on shared characteristics. Cybersecurity researchers analyze the code, behavior, and propagation methods of malware to categorize them into families.

For example, the Zeus banking Trojan and its variants belong to the Zeus malware family. These Trojans share common characteristics and are known for their ability to steal financial information. By classifying malware into families, researchers can identify relationships between different strains, track their evolution, and develop more effective countermeasures.

Another example is the WannaCry ransomware, which is part of the Ransom.WanaCrypt0r family. This classification helps experts understand the ransomware's origins and propagation methods, aiding in the development of decryption tools and prevention strategies.

Classifying malware is an ongoing process, as new strains and variants emerge regularly. Researchers use techniques like code analysis, behavior analysis, and network traffic analysis to uncover the traits that define malware families. This information is vital for developing detection signatures, improving security software, and sharing threat intelligence within the cybersecurity community.

In summary, the classification of malware types and families is like deciphering the many dialects of a digital underworld. Each category and family of malware has its unique characteristics, behaviors, and purposes. By understanding these distinctions, cybersecurity experts can better defend against digital threats, track their evolution, and develop effective countermeasures. This ongoing effort is crucial in the ever-evolving battle to protect our digital domains from the diverse and ever-changing landscape of cyber threats.

Let's embark on a journey into the intricate world of identifying malware, where we'll unravel the telltale signs and behaviors that distinguish these digital adversaries from legitimate software. Think of this as a detective's quest, where we delve into the fascinating clues that reveal the true nature of malware lurking in the digital shadows. Malware, my dear reader, wears many disguises, but it cannot hide its true nature entirely. Just as a skilled detective can spot a criminal amidst a crowd, cybersecurity experts can recognize malware by analyzing its characteristics and behavior.

First and foremost, we look at the file attributes of a suspicious program. It's like examining the physical traits of a suspect in a criminal investigation. Malware often conceals itself using deceptive file names, extensions, or hidden attributes. By scrutinizing these attributes, we can uncover the first clues that point to malicious intent.

Malware often exhibits stealthy behavior, just as a thief tries to move quietly in the night. It may hide its presence by altering system files, disabling security mechanisms, or using rootkit techniques to conceal itself from detection. These evasive tactics raise red flags for cybersecurity experts, who then delve deeper to expose the malware's true nature.

Another key characteristic of malware is its tendency to self-replicate. This behavior is akin to a contagion, where one infected host can spread the malware to others. Viruses and worms are prime examples of this trait. When analyzing malware, cybersecurity experts look for signs of replication, such as modified system files or network activity indicative of spreading.

Malware also displays varying degrees of obfuscation. It's like a criminal covering their tracks with a web of deception. Malicious code may be heavily encrypted, making it challenging to analyze. However, cybersecurity experts use reverse engineering techniques to decode and understand the hidden instructions within the malware.

Behavior analysis plays a significant role in identifying malware. It's akin to observing a suspect's actions to determine their guilt. Malware often exhibits abnormal behaviors, such as unauthorized access to system resources, data exfiltration, or communication with command-and-control servers. These behaviors are glaring indicators of malicious intent.

Network traffic analysis is another crucial tool in identifying malware. Think of it as intercepting coded messages between criminals. When malware communicates with remote servers for commands or data exfiltration, it leaves traces in network traffic. Cybersecurity experts scrutinize these patterns to uncover the presence of malware.

Understanding the malware's communication protocols is essential. It's like deciphering a secret code used by criminals. Malware often uses specific protocols or encryption to communicate with its controllers. By dissecting these protocols, cybersecurity experts can gain insights into the malware's command-and-control infrastructure.

Moreover, malware exhibits various infection vectors. Think of them as entry points for a burglar. Malware can enter a system through email attachments, malicious websites, infected downloads, or removable media. Identifying the infection vector helps cybersecurity experts trace the malware's point of entry and prevent future infections through the same route.

Payload analysis is like uncovering the hidden agenda of a criminal. Malware payloads can include data destruction, data theft, or remote control of a compromised system. By analyzing the payload, cybersecurity experts can determine the malware's objectives and potential impact on the victim's system.

Behavioral analysis extends to examining how malware interacts with the system. It's like watching a suspect's actions after entering a crime scene. Malware may create files, modify registry entries, or spawn malicious processes. By monitoring these interactions, cybersecurity experts can understand the malware's activities and devise countermeasures.

Polymorphism is a tactic used by malware to change its appearance. It's akin to a criminal changing disguises to avoid detection. Polymorphic malware alters its code with each infection, making it challenging to detect using signature-based methods. Cybersecurity experts employ heuristics and behavioral analysis to identify polymorphic malware based on its underlying behavior.

Furthermore, malware often employs evasion techniques to avoid detection by security software. It's like a fugitive constantly changing their route to elude pursuers. Evasion techniques can include code obfuscation, anti-analysis mechanisms, or self-destruct mechanisms. Cybersecurity experts work tirelessly to overcome these evasion tactics and reveal the malware's true nature.

Sandboxing is a controlled environment where suspicious files and programs are executed to observe their behavior. It's like a detective setting up a controlled crime scene to gather evidence. Sandboxing helps cybersecurity experts analyze malware in a safe environment, allowing them to observe its behavior without risking harm to their systems.

In summary, identifying malware characteristics and behavior is a complex but essential aspect of cybersecurity. Just as a detective relies on keen observation and analysis to solve a case, cybersecurity experts rely on a combination of file analysis, behavior analysis, network traffic analysis, and reverse engineering to uncover the true nature of malware. By understanding the traits and behaviors that distinguish malware from legitimate software, experts can develop effective countermeasures to protect digital environments from these digital adversaries. This ongoing detective work is crucial in the ever-evolving battle against cyber threats.

Chapter 3: Setting Up a Malware Analysis Environment

Let's embark on a journey into the intriguing world of building a secure malware analysis lab, where we'll explore the essential steps and considerations required to create a safe environment for dissecting and understanding malicious software. Think of this as setting up a high-tech laboratory for digital detectives, ensuring that they can examine malware without putting their own systems at risk.

Creating a malware analysis lab is akin to establishing a controlled environment for scientific experiments. The first step is to select a dedicated physical or virtual machine that will serve as your analysis workstation. This machine should be isolated from your primary system to prevent any accidental infections or data breaches.

Once you have your analysis workstation, the next crucial step is to install a clean and up-to-date operating system. Think of this as ensuring your lab equipment is in pristine condition. You want a fresh start with no existing infections or vulnerabilities that malware could exploit. Regularly update the operating system and security patches to keep it secure.

Now, it's time to consider the tools of the trade. Malware analysis requires a variety of software tools for different tasks. You'll need a disassembler, debugger, and reverse engineering tools to dissect and analyze malware code. These tools are like the microscopes and instruments in a scientific laboratory, helping you examine the inner workings of malicious software.

In addition to analysis tools, you'll also need sandboxing software. Sandboxes create controlled environments where you can safely execute malware samples and observe their behavior. Think of them as specialized containment chambers in your lab, preventing malware from escaping and causing harm to your system.

Another critical element of your malware analysis lab is network isolation. This means ensuring that your analysis workstation is not connected to your organization's network or the internet. It's like working with hazardous materials in a sealed and secure environment to prevent any accidental contamination.

Consider using a virtual private network (VPN) or a physical air-gapped network to achieve this isolation. This ensures that malware samples cannot communicate with external servers or infect other devices on your network.

Now, let's talk about sample management. In your malware analysis lab, you'll encounter a wide variety of malware samples, each requiring careful handling. You need a system to organize and store these samples securely. Think of it as having labeled containers in your lab to store different types of chemicals. Use a naming convention and storage method that allows you to easily retrieve and reference samples while keeping them isolated.

For added security, consider setting up a separate physical network for your malware analysis lab. This ensures complete isolation from your organization's network, minimizing the risk of accidental infections spreading beyond the lab.

Remember that malware analysis often involves risky operations that could harm your analysis workstation. To mitigate this risk, take regular snapshots or backups of your analysis environment. Think of it as having a safety net to restore your lab setup to a clean state if something goes wrong during analysis.

Now, let's discuss the importance of documentation. In your malware analysis lab, thorough documentation is like keeping a detailed lab notebook. Record your procedures, findings, and observations meticulously. This documentation is invaluable for future reference, knowledge sharing, and ensuring consistency in your analysis. Access control is another crucial aspect of lab security. Limit access to your malware analysis lab to trusted individuals with the necessary skills and permissions. Think of it as having restricted access to a high-security facility. This reduces the risk of unauthorized users accidentally triggering malware samples or compromising your analysis environment.

Consider implementing strong authentication measures, such as multi-factor authentication, to enhance security. Regularly review and update access privileges based on the responsibilities of lab users.

When it comes to sharing your findings, exercise caution. Malware samples can be highly sensitive and dangerous. Sharing them without proper precautions could lead to unintended consequences. Think of it as handling hazardous materials with extreme care. Share findings and samples only with trusted colleagues or within a secure environment designed for this purpose.

Lastly, continuous learning and staying updated on the latest malware threats and analysis techniques are vital. Malware is constantly evolving, and attackers are becoming more sophisticated. Think of it as attending regular training sessions to keep your lab skills sharp. Join online forums and communities where experts share knowledge and insights. In summary, building a secure malware analysis lab is like constructing a high-tech laboratory for digital detectives. It involves setting up an isolated environment, selecting the right tools, ensuring network security, managing samples, documenting procedures, controlling access, and staying informed about the latest threats. By following these steps and maintaining a strong focus on security, you can create a safe and effective workspace for dissecting and understanding malicious software, contributing to the ongoing battle against cyber threats. Imagine stepping into a world where you can dissect and analyze malicious software without risking your physical hardware. This world exists in the form of virtualized environments, where we can create secure and isolated spaces for malware analysis. Think of it as having a laboratory where you can examine digital specimens without the fear of contamination.

Setting up a virtualized environment for malware analysis starts with selecting the right virtualization platform. Think of this as choosing the foundation for your lab. Popular options include VMware, VirtualBox, and Hyper-V. Each has its strengths, but the choice ultimately depends on your specific needs and preferences.

Once you've chosen your virtualization platform, the next step is to create a dedicated virtual machine (VM) for analysis. This VM will serve as your controlled environment, much like a secure containment chamber in a scientific lab. It should have a clean and up-to-date operating system installed, free from any personal or sensitive data.

Consider using a lightweight and easily restorable OS, such as a minimal Linux distribution or a hardened Windows image. Think of it as having a sterile workbench in your lab, ready for experimentation without any pre-existing conditions.

Now, let's talk about snapshots. Snapshots are like checkpoints in your virtualized environment, allowing you to save the current state of your VM. Think of them as bookmarks in your lab notebook, enabling you to return to a known state at any time. Before conducting malware analysis, take a snapshot of your clean VM. This serves as a safety net, allowing you to reset the environment if things go awry during analysis.

Network configuration is crucial in your virtualized environment. Just as you'd establish controlled conditions in a lab, you need to create a network setup that isolates your analysis VM from the rest of your network. Think of it as having a quarantine area within your lab to prevent any accidental spread of contamination.

One effective approach is to use a host-only network or a network bridge, depending on your virtualization platform. These configurations allow your analysis VM to communicate only with specific network segments or other VMs within the same virtualized environment. It's like having a secure containment chamber with controlled access to prevent the escape of any hazardous materials.

Consider using network firewalls or access control lists (ACLs) to further restrict network traffic to and from your analysis VM. Think of this as setting up security barriers within your lab to ensure that only authorized interactions occur.

In addition to network isolation, it's essential to configure your analysis VM with limited resources. Think of this as allocating specific lab equipment for a particular experiment. Limit the amount of CPU, RAM, and storage available to the VM. This prevents resource-intensive malware from overwhelming your virtualized environment.

Snapshot management is a critical aspect of your virtualized lab. Think of it as organizing and labeling your lab materials. Create a systematic approach for naming and managing snapshots to ensure clarity and ease of use. For example, you might use naming conventions that include the date, analysis type, or malware family.

Remember that malware samples can be highly sensitive and dangerous. Treat them with extreme caution, just as you would handle hazardous materials in a lab. Store malware samples in a secure location, and use strong encryption to protect them from unauthorized access.

When conducting malware analysis, always follow best practices for safe handling of samples. Think of it as wearing protective gear in a lab. Use dedicated analysis tools and processes to avoid accidental infections. Isolate your analysis VM from the internet and your organization's network to prevent any unintended consequences.

After completing an analysis, take thorough notes and document your findings. Think of it as keeping detailed records of your experiments. This documentation is invaluable for reference, knowledge sharing, and future analysis. It allows you to track your progress and share insights with colleagues.

Finally, consider the legal and ethical aspects of malware analysis. Just as you'd adhere to ethical guidelines in a scientific lab, ensure that your analysis activities comply with local laws and industry standards. Seek legal advice if needed, and always respect the privacy and rights of individuals and organizations.

In summary, configuring virtualized environments for malware analysis is like creating a secure and controlled laboratory for digital investigations. It involves selecting the right virtualization platform, creating dedicated analysis VMs, taking snapshots for safety, configuring network isolation, managing resources, and handling malware samples with care. By following these best practices and maintaining a strong focus on security and ethics, you can conduct effective and safe malware analysis in your virtualized lab, contributing to the ongoing efforts to combat cyber threats.

Chapter 4: Static Analysis Techniques

Welcome to the fascinating world of analyzing malware binaries and code, where we'll dive deep into the inner workings of malicious software to understand its behavior, capabilities, and intentions. Think of this as a journey into the digital underworld, where we shine a light on the dark corners of the cyber realm.

When it comes to analyzing malware, one of the first steps is acquiring the malicious binary. Think of this as collecting evidence at a crime scene. Malware can be obtained from various sources, including infected systems, phishing emails, or online repositories. Once you have the binary in your possession, it's time to dissect it.

Static analysis is like examining the external appearance of a suspect without any movement. In the context of malware analysis, static analysis involves scrutinizing the binary's code and structure without executing it. Think of it as studying a photograph of a criminal before diving into their criminal activities. Static analysis techniques include examining file headers, identifying code sections, and extracting strings and resources embedded within the binary.

Dynamic analysis, on the other hand, is like observing a suspect's actions and behaviors in real-time. In malware analysis, dynamic analysis involves executing the binary in a controlled environment to observe its behavior. It's akin to monitoring a suspect's movements during a stakeout. Dynamic analysis can reveal how the malware interacts with the system, communicates with external servers, and performs malicious actions.

Disassembling the malware binary is akin to taking apart a complex piece of machinery to understand its components. Disassemblers convert machine code into a more human-readable assembly language. Think of it as translating a foreign language into one you understand. This process allows analysts to examine the binary's instructions and logic in detail.

Reverse engineering is the art of deciphering a malware binary's functionality and intentions. It's like solving a puzzle to reveal the bigger picture. Reverse engineers use various tools and techniques to understand how the malware operates. This includes identifying its algorithms, data structures, and communication protocols.

Decompilation is like translating a text from one language to another to understand its meaning. In malware analysis, decompilers convert compiled code back into a higher-level programming language. This makes it easier for analysts to comprehend the malware's logic and functionality. Think of it as transforming a coded message into plain text.

Code review involves a meticulous examination of the malware's code to uncover vulnerabilities or potential weaknesses. It's like proofreading a document for errors. Code review can reveal flaws that malware authors may have overlooked, which can be valuable information for security professionals.

Behavioral analysis is akin to observing a suspect's actions in a controlled environment. When analyzing malware, behavioral analysis involves executing the binary and monitoring its interactions with the system and network. It's like watching a suspect's movements during an investigation. Behavioral analysis helps uncover the malware's intentions and capabilities.

Sandboxing is a controlled environment where malware binaries can be executed safely. Think of it as a secure testing ground where you can observe the malware's behavior without risking harm to your own system. Sandboxes provide valuable insights into how the malware operates without allowing it to cause real damage.

Network traffic analysis is like intercepting and decoding messages sent by criminals. Malware often communicates with remote servers for commands or data exfiltration. Network traffic analysis allows analysts to trace the malware's communication patterns and identify command-and-control servers.

Pattern recognition is a crucial skill in malware analysis. It's like identifying recurring patterns in a criminal's behavior. Analysts look for common code structures, algorithms, or techniques used by malware authors. Detecting these patterns can help classify the malware and identify its origins.

Malware often employs evasion techniques to avoid detection. It's like a fugitive trying to escape law enforcement. Evasion techniques can include code obfuscation, anti-analysis mechanisms, or self-destruct mechanisms. Analysts must overcome these tactics to fully understand the malware.

Collaboration and knowledge sharing are essential in the world of malware analysis. Think of it as detectives from different agencies pooling their resources to solve a complex case. Analysts often share findings, samples, and insights with colleagues and the broader cybersecurity community to stay ahead of evolving threats.

In summary, analyzing malware binaries and code is a complex but essential aspect of cybersecurity. It involves static and dynamic analysis, disassembly, reverse engineering, decompilation, code review, behavioral analysis, sandboxing, network traffic analysis, pattern recognition, and evasion tactics. By employing these techniques and collaborating with others in the field, analysts can unravel the mysteries of malware, protect systems, and contribute to the ongoing battle against cyber threats.

Let's embark on a journey into the world of identifying Indicators of Compromise (IOCs), a crucial skill in the realm of cybersecurity. Think of this as developing a keen sense of detecting subtle clues, like a seasoned detective investigating a complex case.

Indicators of Compromise, or IOCs, are pieces of evidence that suggest a system has been compromised by malicious activity. Imagine these as the telltale signs that something suspicious is happening. They can manifest in various forms, and cybersecurity professionals are like detectives who use these clues to uncover hidden threats.

One common type of IOC is a file hash, which is like a digital fingerprint. By calculating the hash of a file, you can create a unique identifier for that file. Think of it as tagging an object with an individual mark. If the same file appears on multiple systems, the hash remains constant, making it easier to detect malicious files.

Another essential IOC is network traffic patterns. Just as detectives track suspects' movements, cybersecurity professionals monitor network traffic to spot irregularities. Unusual traffic, such as unexpected connections to suspicious IP addresses or uncommon data transfer patterns, can be indicators of compromise.

Login anomalies are akin to noticing unusual behavior in a suspect's routine. When users log into systems, their activity leaves traces. Unexpected login attempts, failed logins, or successful logins from unexpected locations can be signs of unauthorized access and potential compromise.

System log anomalies are like examining a suspect's alibi for inconsistencies. System logs record events and actions on a computer. Anomalies in these logs, such as deleted or altered entries, can be indications of tampering or intrusion.

Malware artifacts are like finding fingerprints at a crime scene. When malware infects a system, it often leaves traces, such as registry entries, files, or system changes. Identifying these artifacts can lead to the discovery of compromised systems.

Phishing emails and malicious attachments are like suspicious letters in an investigation. Cybercriminals often use phishing emails to deliver malware or steal credentials. Detecting these phishing attempts and analyzing their content is crucial in identifying IOCs.

Domain and URL analysis is akin to tracing a suspect's online activities. Malicious domains or URLs can lead to compromised systems. Identifying suspicious domains or URLs and monitoring their activity is essential for IOC detection.

Behavioral anomalies are like noticing unusual behavior in a suspect's daily routine. Malware can change system behavior, leading to unexpected actions. Detecting these behavioral anomalies can help identify compromised systems.

Registry changes are like finding hidden compartments in a suspect's residence. Malware often alters the Windows Registry to maintain persistence. Detecting unauthorized registry changes is essential for IOC identification.

Now, let's discuss the importance of threat intelligence feeds. Think of these as informants providing valuable tips to detectives. Threat intelligence feeds provide up-to-date information on known threats, including IOCs. Cybersecurity professionals can subscribe to these feeds to stay informed about emerging threats and known indicators of compromise.

Continuous monitoring is crucial in identifying IOCs promptly. Just as detectives keep a watchful eye on a suspect, cybersecurity professionals must monitor systems and networks for any signs of compromise. Automated tools can assist in real-time IOC detection and response.

Incident response plans are like having a well-prepared strategy for handling a crisis. In the event of a suspected compromise, organizations should have documented incident response procedures in place. These plans outline how to investigate and mitigate potential IOCs effectively.

Sharing threat intelligence is akin to law enforcement agencies cooperating to solve complex cases. Cybersecurity professionals and organizations should actively share IOCs and threat intelligence with trusted partners and industry peers. This collaborative approach strengthens the collective defense against cyber threats.

Machine learning and artificial intelligence are like having advanced forensic tools at your disposal. These technologies can analyze vast amounts of data and identify subtle patterns that may indicate compromise. Incorporating machine learning into IOC detection enhances the speed and accuracy of threat identification.

Data correlation is akin to connecting the dots in an investigation. Cybersecurity professionals use data correlation techniques to combine multiple sources of information and identify IOCs that may not be apparent when analyzed individually. This holistic approach improves the detection of complex threats.

Timeliness is critical in IOC detection. Just as detectives act quickly to apprehend a suspect, cybersecurity professionals must respond promptly to potential indicators of compromise. Rapid identification and mitigation can minimize the impact of a security incident.

Regular IOC hunting is like conducting proactive surveillance in a high-crime area. Cybersecurity teams should actively search for IOCs within their networks, even in the absence of specific alerts. This proactive approach helps uncover threats before they cause significant damage.

False positives are akin to mistakenly identifying an innocent person as a suspect. IOC detection tools may generate false alarms. Cybersecurity professionals must carefully investigate these alerts to distinguish between real threats and false positives.

In summary, identifying Indicators of Compromise (IOCs) is a fundamental aspect of cybersecurity, akin to detective work in the digital realm. It involves recognizing various signs, such as file hashes, network traffic patterns, login anomalies, system log irregularities, malware artifacts, and more. Cybersecurity professionals rely on threat intelligence feeds, continuous monitoring, incident response plans, collaboration, advanced technologies, data correlation, and timely actions to effectively detect and respond to IOCs. By mastering the art of IOC identification, cybersecurity teams can safeguard their organizations from threats and maintain a strong defense against cyberattacks.

Chapter 5: Dynamic Analysis Methods

Welcome to the intriguing world of behavioral analysis in controlled environments—a realm where we examine the actions and reactions of software, much like studying the behavior of living organisms in a controlled laboratory setting. Think of this as observing the unique characteristics and tendencies of digital entities to understand their intentions and impact.

Behavioral analysis is like setting up a controlled experiment in a laboratory. In cybersecurity, it involves executing software or files in a secure and isolated environment to observe their behavior. This behavior can provide valuable insights into whether the software is benign or malicious.

Think of this analysis as watching a play unfold on a stage. The software, like actors, follows a script or set of instructions as it interacts with the environment. Behavioral analysis allows us to monitor these interactions and actions, helping us identify any suspicious or harmful behavior.

One key aspect of behavioral analysis is the use of sandbox environments. These environments are isolated and controlled spaces where software can be executed safely. Think of them as sealed chambers in a laboratory, preventing any potential harm from escaping and affecting the rest of the system.

In a sandbox, the software is free to perform its actions without posing any risk to the host system. This controlled setup allows us to closely monitor and record everything the software does, from file changes and registry modifications to network communication and system calls.

Behavioral analysis goes beyond static analysis, which examines the software's code and structure without execution. Think of static analysis as analyzing the blueprint of a building without seeing how it functions. While static analysis provides valuable insights, behavioral analysis offers a real-world view of how software behaves when running.

When a suspicious file or software is introduced into the sandbox, it's like introducing a new species into a controlled ecosystem. We carefully observe how it interacts with the environment, other files, and the system as a whole. This allows us to detect any unusual or malicious behavior.

An important aspect of behavioral analysis is defining what constitutes normal behavior. Think of this as establishing a baseline for expected actions. By understanding how legitimate software typically behaves, we can more easily spot deviations and anomalies that may indicate a threat.

Behavioral analysis tools and sandboxes use a variety of techniques to capture and analyze behavior. This includes monitoring system calls, tracking file system changes, logging network activity, and recording interactions with system resources. These observations are like the notes taken by a scientist during an experiment.

One crucial benefit of behavioral analysis is its ability to detect previously unknown threats or zero-day vulnerabilities. Think of this as being prepared for a new, unknown disease in a medical lab. Since behavioral analysis focuses on behavior rather than known signatures, it can identify threats that traditional antivirus software might miss.

Behavioral analysis can also provide valuable insights into the tactics, techniques, and procedures (TTPs) employed by cybercriminals. Think of this as studying the hunting behaviors of predators in the wild. By understanding how malware behaves, cybersecurity professionals can develop better defenses and responses.

However, behavioral analysis is not without its challenges. Just as observing animal behavior in the wild can be unpredictable, analyzing software behavior can be complex. Malware often employs evasion techniques to hide its true intentions, such as delaying malicious actions or mimicking legitimate behavior.

False positives are like mistaking a harmless creature for a predator in the wild. Behavioral analysis tools may sometimes flag legitimate software as suspicious due to certain behaviors. Cybersecurity professionals must carefully investigate these alerts to avoid unnecessary alarm.

Behavioral analysis is an evolving field, much like scientific research that constantly discovers new phenomena. Cybercriminals are continually adapting their tactics, which means that behavioral analysis techniques must also evolve to keep pace.

In summary, behavioral analysis in controlled environments is a vital tool in the cybersecurity arsenal, akin to conducting experiments in a controlled laboratory. It involves observing the behavior of software in a sandbox environment to detect suspicious or malicious actions. By closely monitoring and analyzing these behaviors, cybersecurity professionals gain valuable insights into the nature of threats and can develop more effective defenses. Just as scientists continually explore the natural world, cybersecurity experts must adapt and refine their behavioral analysis techniques to stay ahead of evolving cyber threats.

Welcome to the dynamic and ever-evolving world of dynamic code execution and monitoring—a realm where we delve into the real-time behavior of software, much like watching a live performance to understand its actions and intentions. Think of this as the art of closely observing digital entities in action to uncover their secrets and behaviors.

Dynamic code execution is like a live theater performance. In the world of cybersecurity, it involves running software or code in a controlled environment to witness its behavior as it unfolds. This real-time observation is akin to attending a play to understand the characters' motivations and actions.

Imagine dynamic code execution as a theater stage where the software performs its script. Here, we have a controlled environment that allows us to closely monitor every action the software takes, from reading and writing files to making system calls and interacting with external resources.

The controlled environment in dynamic code execution is often referred to as a sandbox, much like the enclosed space where a play is performed. The sandbox provides a safe and isolated space where software can be executed without posing any risk to the host system. This controlled setting allows us to observe the software's actions without fear of it causing harm.

Dynamic code execution differs from static analysis, which involves examining the software's code and structure without execution. Think of static analysis as studying a script or screenplay without seeing the actors in action. While static analysis provides valuable insights, dynamic execution offers a real-world view of how the software behaves when running.

In dynamic code execution, we carefully watch as the software interacts with the environment, just as an audience watches actors on stage. We observe how it reads and writes files, makes registry changes, communicates over the network, and performs other actions. This real-time monitoring helps us uncover any suspicious or malicious behavior.

To perform dynamic code execution effectively, we must define what constitutes normal behavior, much like understanding the expected actions of characters in a play. By establishing a baseline for legitimate software behavior, we can more easily identify deviations and anomalies that may indicate a threat.

Dynamic code execution tools and sandboxes use various techniques to capture and analyze behavior.

They monitor system calls, track file system changes, log network activity, and record interactions with system resources. These observations are like the notes taken by a director during a live performance.

One of the key benefits of dynamic code execution is its ability to detect previously unknown threats or zero-day vulnerabilities. Think of it as being prepared for an unexpected twist in a play. Since dynamic analysis focuses on behavior rather than known signatures, it can identify threats that traditional antivirus software might miss.

Dynamic code execution also provides valuable insights into the tactics, techniques, and procedures (TTPs) used by cybercriminals. Much like understanding the motives and actions of characters in a story, analyzing malware behavior helps cybersecurity professionals develop better defenses and responses.

However, dynamic code execution is not without its challenges. Just as unexpected plot twists can confound an audience, malware often employs evasion techniques to hide its true intentions. This can include delaying malicious actions, encrypting communication, or mimicking legitimate behavior.

False positives in dynamic code execution are like mistaking an actor's improvisation for a scripted line. Tools may sometimes flag legitimate software as suspicious due to certain behaviors. Cybersecurity professionals must carefully investigate these alerts to avoid unnecessary alarm.

The field of dynamic code execution is continually evolving, much like the world of theater, which constantly explores new genres and styles. As cyber threats become more sophisticated, dynamic analysis techniques must adapt to detect and respond to emerging threats effectively.

In summary, dynamic code execution and monitoring are invaluable tools in the cybersecurity arsenal, akin to watching a live performance to understand the characters' motivations and actions. It involves running software in a controlled environment to observe its behavior in real-time. By closely monitoring and analyzing these behaviors, cybersecurity professionals gain critical insights into the nature of threats and can develop more effective defenses. Just as theater evolves to tell new stories, dynamic analysis techniques must adapt to stay ahead of ever-evolving cyber threats.

Chapter 6: Signature-Based Detection with YARA

Welcome to the world of YARA signatures—an essential tool in the cybersecurity toolkit that empowers us to identify and detect specific patterns and characteristics in files or code. Think of YARA signatures as the digital fingerprints that help us recognize and classify malware and other digital entities.

Imagine you're an investigator in a vast library, searching for books with specific characteristics. YARA signatures are like the guidelines or criteria you follow to identify those books. They're a set of rules and patterns that tell us what to look for in the digital realm.

YARA signatures are powerful because they allow us to automate the process of pattern recognition. Instead of manually inspecting every file, we can create rules that define the unique features we're interested in. It's like having a detective with a magnifying glass who can quickly spot clues that match a predefined pattern.

These signatures are incredibly versatile. They can be used to detect malware, analyze documents, identify file formats, and even uncover specific behaviors or characteristics within code. Think of them as adaptable tools that can be applied to a wide range of digital investigations.

YARA signatures are akin to the fingerprints used in criminal investigations. Just as each person has unique fingerprints, files and code have distinct patterns and characteristics. YARA allows us to define and search for these patterns efficiently.

To create a YARA signature, we need to specify the conditions that must be met for a match to occur. It's like writing a set of rules for a board game—each rule describes a specific aspect we're interested in. These rules can encompass strings, regular expressions, and Boolean conditions.

Strings in YARA signatures are like keywords or phrases we're looking for in a text. Imagine you're searching for mentions of a particular topic in a book—the strings in a YARA signature are the specific words or phrases you're searching for. When YARA finds a match, it's like discovering that specific keyword in the text.

Regular expressions in YARA signatures are like search patterns that can match a range of variations. For example, if you're looking for all words that start with "cyber," you can use a regular expression to define that pattern. YARA will then identify any word that fits that pattern, just as a detective might look for words with a certain prefix.

Boolean conditions in YARA signatures allow us to create complex rules. Imagine you're investigating a case with multiple criteria. Boolean conditions are like saying, "I want to find books that are both detective stories and set in the 19th century." YARA allows us to combine conditions to create precise and flexible rules.

One of the strengths of YARA is its ability to identify both known and unknown threats. Known threats are like books with well-documented contents—you can create YARA signatures based on their known characteristics. However, YARA can also help uncover unknown threats by identifying patterns that deviate from the norm.

YARA signatures can be shared and distributed within the cybersecurity community, much like sharing investigative techniques with fellow detectives. This collaborative approach enhances the collective defense against cyber threats. When one cybersecurity professional discovers a new pattern or threat, they can create a YARA signature and share it with others.

YARA is not limited to static analysis—it can also be used for dynamic analysis, just as a detective might use different tools and techniques for various aspects of an investigation. By applying YARA signatures to real-time monitoring, we can detect and respond to threats as they unfold.

False positives in YARA signatures are like mistaking a book for something it's not. Sometimes, a YARA signature may match a file or code that resembles a threat but isn't malicious. Cybersecurity professionals must carefully tune and validate their YARA signatures to reduce false alarms.

YARA signatures are continually evolving, much like the techniques and tools used in investigations. As cyber threats become more sophisticated, YARA rules must adapt to detect and identify new patterns and characteristics.

In summary, YARA signatures are a vital tool in the cybersecurity landscape, akin to a detective's toolkit for pattern recognition. They allow us to define specific patterns and characteristics in files or code, enabling us to efficiently identify and classify digital entities. YARA signatures are versatile, adaptable, and essential for both known and unknown threat detection. By sharing these signatures and collaborating with fellow cybersecurity professionals, we strengthen our collective defense against cyber threats. As the digital landscape evolves, so too must our YARA signatures to keep pace with emerging threats.

Welcome to the fascinating world of creating custom YARA rules for malware detection—a skill that empowers you to craft your own digital detective scripts to identify and catch malicious software. Think of custom YARA rules as the unique lenses through which you examine the digital landscape, enabling you to spot the telltale signs of malware and other digital threats.

Imagine you're a chef in a kitchen, creating your own recipes. Custom YARA rules are like your secret ingredients, carefully selected to add flavor and uniqueness to your dishes. These rules are your way of defining what is and isn't acceptable in the world of digital files and code.

Creating custom YARA rules is akin to crafting a set of guidelines for your own treasure hunt. You're setting the criteria and clues that will lead you to discovering malicious files or code. Just like a treasure hunter selects specific tools and strategies, you're choosing the characteristics and patterns that matter most to your investigation.

One of the great advantages of crafting custom YARA rules is the ability to tailor them to your specific needs. Think of it as having a tailor-made suit that fits you perfectly. While generic rules are useful, custom rules allow you to focus on the unique aspects of your environment, applications, or threats.

Custom YARA rules are like your personal filters for the digital world. You can decide what types of files, code, or behaviors you want to target. It's as if you're saying, "I'm interested in finding files that exhibit these specific traits." With your custom rules, you become the curator of your digital collection.

The process of creating custom YARA rules often starts with defining the characteristics you want to detect. These characteristics can include unique strings, patterns, or behaviors that are indicative of malware. Think of it as describing the traits you're looking for in a suspect.

Strings in custom YARA rules are like the keywords you use to search for something specific online. You're identifying specific words, phrases, or sequences of characters that are associated with malicious software. When YARA finds a match, it's like uncovering a hidden clue in an investigation.

Regular expressions in custom YARA rules are your advanced search patterns. They allow you to define complex, flexible, and dynamic criteria. It's as if you're saying, "I want to find anything that matches this pattern, regardless of variations." This versatility can be especially valuable when dealing with polymorphic malware.

Boolean conditions in custom YARA rules allow you to create complex logic. It's like setting up rules for a board game with multiple conditions that must be met. These conditions can involve combinations of strings, regular expressions, and logical operators, enabling you to create precise and nuanced rules.

Custom YARA rules are like having your own personal sniffer dog trained to detect a specific scent. You're training YARA to recognize the scent of malware by defining its unique odor, so to speak. Once YARA has learned to detect that scent, it can sniff out malicious files or code with remarkable accuracy.

Creating custom YARA rules requires a deep understanding of both malware characteristics and YARA's syntax and capabilities. It's like mastering a craft that combines art and science. The more you practice and refine your skills, the better you become at crafting effective rules.

False positives in custom YARA rules are like mistaking a friendly face for a foe. Sometimes, a rule may inadvertently flag a legitimate file or code as malicious due to a resemblance in characteristics. This is why crafting and fine-tuning custom rules is both an art and a science, requiring careful consideration.

Sharing custom YARA rules with the cybersecurity community is like sharing your detective techniques with fellow investigators. Collaboration in creating and refining rules enhances the collective defense against malware and other digital threats. Just as detectives share insights and methods, cybersecurity professionals can benefit from each other's expertise.

In summary, creating custom YARA rules for malware detection is a powerful skill that allows you to define your own criteria for identifying digital threats. These rules are your digital detectives, carefully crafted to spot the unique characteristics of malware in your environment. Custom rules offer flexibility, precision, and the ability to focus on specific aspects of your investigation. As you develop and share your custom rules, you contribute to the collective effort to protect digital landscapes from malicious software. Like a seasoned detective, you refine your skills and techniques, adapting to the evolving world of cyber threats.

Chapter 7: Behavioral Analysis and Sandboxing

Welcome to the intriguing realm of behavioral analysis in malware detection—a topic that takes us deep into the behaviors and actions of digital entities, much like watching the moves of characters in a thrilling movie. Think of behavioral analysis as the art of observing software's actions in real-time to discern whether it's a hero or a villain in the digital world.

Behavioral analysis is like attending a live theater performance where you watch actors' every move to understand their motives and intentions. In cybersecurity, this involves closely monitoring software's actions as it runs, much as you would scrutinize the actions of actors on stage.

Imagine behavioral analysis as an investigation into the actions and behaviors of software, just as detectives study the actions and motives of suspects. Here, we're not concerned with the source code but rather the actual behaviors exhibited by the software when executed.

The key to behavioral analysis is real-time observation—much like a wildlife biologist observing animals in their natural habitat. We watch as the software interacts with the environment, making file changes, system calls, and network communications. This real-time monitoring helps us uncover any suspicious or malicious behavior.

Behavioral analysis is not limited to static analysis, where we examine code without execution. It's dynamic, like watching a live performance to understand the characters' motivations and actions. While static analysis provides valuable insights, dynamic analysis offers a real-world view of how the software behaves when running.

In behavioral analysis, we establish a baseline for normal behavior, akin to understanding the expected actions of characters in a story. By defining what's typical, we can more readily spot deviations and anomalies that may signal a threat.

The tools used in behavioral analysis are like surveillance cameras that capture every move of the software. They monitor system calls, track file system changes, log network activity, and record interactions with system resources. These observations are like the notes taken by a director during a live performance.

One of the strengths of behavioral analysis is its ability to detect previously unknown threats or zero-day vulnerabilities. Think of it as being prepared for an unexpected twist in a story. Since behavioral analysis focuses on behavior rather than known signatures, it can identify threats that traditional antivirus software might miss.

Behavioral analysis also provides insights into the tactics, techniques, and procedures (TTPs) used by cybercriminals. Much like understanding the motives and actions of characters in a movie, analyzing malware behavior helps cybersecurity professionals develop better defenses and responses.

However, behavioral analysis is not without its challenges. Just as unexpected plot twists can confound an audience, malware often employs evasion techniques to hide its true intentions. This can include delaying malicious actions, encrypting communication, or mimicking legitimate behavior.

False positives in behavioral analysis are like mistaking an actor's improvisation for a scripted line. Tools may sometimes flag legitimate software as suspicious due to certain behaviors. Cybersecurity professionals must carefully investigate these alerts to avoid unnecessary alarm.

The field of behavioral analysis is continually evolving, much like the world of cinema, which explores new genres and storytelling techniques. As cyber threats become more sophisticated, behavioral analysis techniques must adapt to detect and respond to emerging threats effectively.

In summary, behavioral analysis in malware detection is a powerful tool that allows us to observe the actions and behaviors of software in real-time. It's akin to watching a live performance to understand the characters' motivations and actions. By closely monitoring and analyzing these behaviors, cybersecurity professionals gain critical insights into the nature of threats and can develop more effective defenses. Just as cinema evolves to tell new stories, behavioral analysis techniques must adapt to stay ahead of ever-evolving cyber threats.

Welcome to the world of sandboxing techniques for dynamic analysis—a fascinating realm where we create safe environments to study the behavior of potentially malicious software, much like conducting experiments in a controlled laboratory. Think of sandboxing as our way of observing how software behaves when unleashed in a secure, controlled space.

Imagine a sandbox as a protective play area for children, where they can explore and interact with toys without risks. In the world of cybersecurity, a sandbox is a similar concept—it's an isolated environment where we can execute and observe software without endangering our real systems.

Sandboxing techniques are like controlled experiments in a laboratory, where scientists carefully study the behavior of elements in a controlled environment. In cybersecurity, we use these techniques to study how software behaves when executed, without exposing our actual systems to potential threats.

Think of sandboxing as a digital playground for software. Here, we can let suspicious or unknown programs run and play, all while monitoring their activities closely. It's like giving a new toy to a child but watching to ensure they don't cause any harm.

Sandboxing is a form of dynamic analysis, much like observing how an athlete performs during a live game. In this case, we're not concerned with the software's source code but rather its real-time actions and interactions with the sandboxed environment.

One of the primary goals of sandboxing is to understand how software interacts with its surroundings. It's like studying the behavior of a new pet to ensure it doesn't disrupt your household. We want to know if the software exhibits any malicious or suspicious behavior.

Sandboxing tools are like the walls of our digital playground, ensuring that the software's actions are contained within a controlled environment. These tools simulate an isolated system, complete with its own file system, registry, and network, allowing us to study software behavior without risk.

The heart of sandboxing is real-time monitoring—much like keeping a close eye on a pet to ensure it doesn't cause any trouble. We watch as the software makes system calls, alters files, communicates over the network, and performs other actions, recording everything for analysis.

Sandboxing is not a one-size-fits-all approach; it's versatile and adaptable, allowing us to customize the environment and the level of monitoring. It's like tailoring a play area for different types of toys and activities, ensuring that we can effectively analyze various software.

One of the strengths of sandboxing is its ability to detect and analyze zero-day threats—much like a scientist discovering a new species in the wild. Since sandboxing focuses on behavior rather than known signatures, it can identify previously unknown and emerging threats.

However, sandboxing is not without its challenges. Just as a child may try to outsmart the rules of a playground, malware often employs evasion techniques to bypass sandboxes. This can include detecting the presence of a sandbox or delaying malicious actions until it's in a real environment.

False negatives in sandboxing are like overlooking a child's misbehavior on the playground. Sometimes, sandboxing tools may miss malicious behavior, leading to a false sense of security. This is why cybersecurity professionals must combine sandboxing with other analysis techniques.

Sharing sandboxing results and techniques within the cybersecurity community is like comparing notes with fellow researchers. Collaboration enhances our collective ability to analyze and respond to threats. Just as scientists share findings to advance knowledge, cybersecurity professionals share insights to improve defenses.

In summary, sandboxing techniques for dynamic analysis provide a safe and controlled environment to study the behavior of potentially malicious software. It's like a digital playground where we let software run and observe its actions closely. By monitoring real-time behavior in a controlled environment, we gain insights into potential threats and can better protect our systems. Sandbox techniques are versatile, adaptable, and valuable in detecting emerging threats, although they must be used in conjunction with other analysis methods to ensure comprehensive security. Like scientists collaborating to advance knowledge, cybersecurity professionals share findings to strengthen our collective defense against cyber threats.

Chapter 8: Incident Response Strategies

Welcome to the essential topic of developing an effective incident response plan—a crucial aspect of cybersecurity that ensures you're well-prepared to handle unexpected events, much like having a fire escape plan for your digital world. Think of an incident response plan as your playbook for tackling cyber threats and minimizing their impact.

Creating an incident response plan is similar to designing a blueprint for a sturdy and resilient building. It's your way of outlining the steps and strategies necessary to protect your digital assets and respond swiftly to any security incidents that may occur.

Consider incident response as your cybersecurity emergency kit, equipped with tools and procedures to address unforeseen challenges. Just as you have a first aid kit at home for physical emergencies, an incident response plan is your toolkit for addressing digital emergencies.

In the world of incident response, preparation is key— much like practicing fire drills to ensure everyone knows what to do in case of a fire. An effective plan defines roles and responsibilities, so your team can respond efficiently when an incident occurs.

Incident response is like having a dedicated team of firefighters ready to extinguish any digital blaze. Your incident response team is equipped with the knowledge and tools to handle a wide range of cybersecurity incidents, from minor incidents to major breaches.

One of the cornerstones of incident response is the identification phase—much like a detective gathering evidence at a crime scene. In this phase, you aim to recognize and assess potential security incidents by monitoring for signs of compromise.

Just as firefighters use specialized equipment to extinguish fires, your incident response team relies on various tools and technologies to investigate and mitigate cyber threats. These tools help you analyze and contain incidents effectively.

The containment phase of incident response is akin to isolating a contagious patient to prevent the spread of disease. Here, the goal is to limit the impact of the incident and prevent further damage.

Incident response also involves eradicating the root cause of the incident, much like eliminating the source of an outbreak to prevent its recurrence. This phase ensures that the vulnerabilities or weaknesses that led to the incident are addressed.

Once the incident is under control, it's essential to focus on recovery, just as a business rebuilds after a disaster. This phase involves restoring affected systems and services to their normal state, minimizing downtime.

Testing your incident response plan is like running fire drills to ensure everyone knows their role and can respond effectively. Regular testing and simulations help identify weaknesses in your plan and allow for continuous improvement.

Documentation is a critical aspect of incident response, much like keeping records of medical treatments. Proper documentation ensures that you can learn from past incidents and make necessary adjustments to your plan.

Incident response is not just about reacting to threats; it's also about learning from each incident to improve your overall security posture. By analyzing incidents and conducting post-incident reviews, you gain valuable insights into potential weaknesses and areas for enhancement.

Incident response is a collaborative effort, much like a team of firefighters working together to extinguish a blaze. Effective communication within your incident response team and with external stakeholders is crucial for a swift and coordinated response.

Sharing incident information with relevant authorities and organizations is akin to alerting the authorities about a fire. It helps law enforcement and other entities take appropriate actions and contribute to the resolution of the incident.

A well-documented incident response plan is like a detailed map that guides you through challenging terrain. It ensures that you can navigate the complex landscape of cybersecurity incidents with confidence and precision.

In summary, developing an effective incident response plan is essential for safeguarding your digital assets and responding swiftly to cybersecurity incidents. Just as you have an emergency kit for physical emergencies, an incident response plan is your digital emergency toolkit. It involves preparation, identification, containment, eradication, recovery, and continuous improvement. Like firefighters working together to extinguish a blaze, your incident response team collaborates to address threats efficiently. Through proper documentation and post-incident analysis, you enhance your overall cybersecurity posture and resilience. An effective incident response plan is your blueprint for success in the ever-evolving landscape of cybersecurity.

Welcome to the critical topic of incident containment and eradication strategies—a pivotal phase in incident response where we focus on stopping the threat and ensuring it doesn't return, much like eliminating the root cause of a persistent illness. Think of it as the crucial step in resolving a cybersecurity incident and preventing future occurrences.

Incident containment is like isolating a contagious patient to prevent the spread of a disease. In cybersecurity, containment involves limiting the damage caused by the incident and preventing it from spreading further throughout your network or systems.

Containment is an immediate response, much like administering first aid to a person in distress. It requires swift action to prevent the incident from escalating and causing more harm.

Just as firefighters work diligently to contain a blaze, your incident response team must work tirelessly to prevent the incident from spreading to other parts of your network or organization. This involves isolating affected systems, restricting access, and stopping malicious activities in their tracks.

During the containment phase, it's essential to gather information and evidence, much like collecting data at a crime scene. This information will be valuable for further analysis and investigation, helping you understand how the incident occurred and what vulnerabilities were exploited.

Once the incident is contained, the focus shifts to eradication—a phase akin to eliminating the source of an outbreak to prevent its recurrence. Here, you aim to identify and remove the root cause of the incident, such as a malware infection or a compromised account.

Eradication involves not only removing the malicious elements but also addressing the underlying vulnerabilities that allowed the incident to occur. It's like fixing a hole in the roof after a rainstorm to prevent future leaks.

Think of eradication as a thorough cleansing process, much like sanitizing a kitchen after a foodborne illness outbreak. You want to ensure that all traces of the threat are eliminated and that your systems are secure once more.

Eradication may involve patching software vulnerabilities, changing passwords, and updating security configurations. It's a comprehensive effort to strengthen your defenses and prevent similar incidents from happening again.

During the eradication phase, it's crucial to document all actions taken, like keeping records of medical treatments. Documentation ensures that you have a clear record of what was done, which can be valuable for post-incident analysis and reporting.

Eradication is a collaborative effort, much like a team of experts working together to solve a complex problem.

Your incident response team, IT staff, and cybersecurity professionals must work cohesively to identify and address vulnerabilities effectively.

Once eradication is complete, it's essential to monitor your systems closely to ensure that the threat doesn't return, much like conducting follow-up medical tests after an illness. Continuous monitoring helps detect any signs of reinfection or new vulnerabilities.

Eradication is not a one-time effort but an ongoing process, similar to maintaining good health through regular exercise and a balanced diet. Your organization must continuously update its security measures and practices to stay resilient against evolving threats.

Collaboration with external organizations and authorities can be beneficial during the containment and eradication phases, much like seeking expert advice when dealing with a complex medical issue. Law enforcement agencies and cybersecurity experts may provide valuable assistance and insights.

In summary, incident containment and eradication strategies are crucial components of incident response, focused on stopping threats and preventing their return. Containment involves swift action to limit the incident's impact and prevent it from spreading further. Eradication is about identifying and removing the root cause of the incident and addressing underlying vulnerabilities. It requires collaboration, documentation, and continuous monitoring to ensure your systems are secure. Just as healthcare professionals work together to treat patients and prevent illnesses, your incident response team and cybersecurity experts collaborate to protect your digital environment. Incident containment and eradication are ongoing efforts to maintain a robust cybersecurity posture in the face of evolving threats.

Chapter 9: Network-Based Malware Detection

Welcome to the intriguing world of network traffic analysis for malware detection—a realm where we dissect the digital traffic flowing through our networks to identify potential threats, much like investigators sifting through evidence to solve a complex case. Think of it as a way to understand the conversations happening within your network and spot any suspicious or malicious activities.

Network traffic analysis is like having surveillance cameras installed throughout your city to monitor and identify criminal behavior. In the digital landscape, we deploy tools and techniques to observe the traffic passing through our network, allowing us to identify any anomalies or signs of malware.

Consider your network as a bustling city with data packets traveling through its streets. Network traffic analysis is akin to having traffic cops who scrutinize the behavior of each packet to ensure it's not causing trouble. We're looking for signs of malicious intent, much like police officers watching for suspicious activities.

Network traffic analysis operates in real-time, similar to how security personnel monitor a live event for any signs of trouble. It's not just about historical data; it's about identifying threats as they occur and responding promptly.

Think of network traffic analysis as a language that helps you understand the conversations happening within your network. By examining the flow of data packets, you can decipher who's talking, what they're saying, and whether it's legitimate or potentially harmful.

Network traffic analysis tools are like interpreters that translate the language of data packets into understandable information. These tools help you make sense of the vast amount of data flowing through your network and highlight anything suspicious.

One of the primary goals of network traffic analysis is to detect anomalies, much like a radar system spotting unusual aircraft movements. Anomalies can be indicators of malware or unauthorized activities, and they often stand out when compared to normal network behavior.

Network traffic analysis also involves identifying patterns of behavior, similar to recognizing a familiar face in a crowd. By understanding how your network typically operates, you can spot deviations that may signal a security threat.

Traffic analysis is like scrutinizing the behavior of people in a crowded marketplace. You're looking for any individuals who stand out due to their suspicious actions, such as trying to pickpocket or engage in other illicit activities.

Just as security personnel in a marketplace would intervene to stop a crime in progress, network traffic analysis allows you to take action when you detect malicious behavior. This might involve blocking a specific IP address or isolating a compromised device.

Timeliness is crucial in network traffic analysis, similar to responding quickly to a security incident to minimize damage. The faster you detect and respond to a threat, the less harm it can cause.

Network traffic analysis is not just about identifying threats but also understanding their scope and impact, much like investigating a crime scene to determine the extent of the damage. This information helps you make informed decisions on how to mitigate the threat.

Collaboration is essential in network traffic analysis, much like law enforcement agencies working together to solve a complex case. Sharing threat intelligence and insights with other organizations can help bolster collective cybersecurity defenses.

In summary, network traffic analysis for malware detection is a vital aspect of cybersecurity, allowing you to monitor the conversations happening within your network and spot potential threats. It's like having digital traffic cops who scrutinize data packets for signs of trouble in real-time. By detecting anomalies and patterns, you can identify and respond to security threats promptly. Collaboration and sharing threat intelligence enhance your ability to protect your network effectively. Network traffic analysis is your surveillance system, your language interpreter, and your tool for maintaining a secure digital environment.

Welcome to the fascinating realm of Intrusion Detection Systems (IDS) and their pivotal role in enhancing network security—a bit like having vigilant security guards in your digital castle, constantly on the lookout for potential threats. IDS is an essential component of modern cybersecurity, serving as the sentinels of your network, detecting and alerting you to any suspicious activities.

Imagine IDS as the watchful guardians of a medieval fortress, standing at the gates, and watching for any signs of an impending attack. They are trained to recognize the tactics and behaviors of potential adversaries, much like IDS are designed to identify patterns associated with cyberattacks.

Your network is like a thriving city with data flowing like traffic on its streets. IDS serve as traffic cops, directing and monitoring this data flow, and intervening if they detect anything amiss. Their mission is to ensure that the digital traffic is safe and secure.

IDS is all about real-time monitoring, much like having CCTV cameras that provide live feeds of your premises. They constantly analyze network traffic, looking for anomalies that could indicate a security breach.

Consider IDS as detectives investigating a crime scene. They collect and analyze evidence, piecing together the puzzle of what happened and identifying any potential threats, such as unauthorized access or suspicious behavior. Intrusion Detection Systems are equipped with specialized tools and techniques, much like forensic investigators have their kits for analyzing evidence. These tools help IDS sift through the vast amount of network data and identify potential security incidents.

One of the primary functions of IDS is to detect anomalies in network traffic, similar to a radar system identifying unusual aircraft movements. Anomalies could be indicators of an attack or malicious activity, and they stand out when compared to normal network behavior.

IDS also play the role of pattern recognition experts, akin to recognizing a familiar face in a crowd. By understanding the typical traffic patterns within your network, IDS can quickly spot deviations that may signal a security threat.

Think of IDS as vigilant sentinels watching over a busy marketplace. They are on the lookout for any individuals who display suspicious behavior, such as attempting to break into a store or engage in other illicit activities.

When IDS detect a potential threat, they don't just stand by—they act. Similar to security personnel intervening to prevent a crime, IDS can trigger alerts, block suspicious traffic, or take other preventive actions.

Timeliness is crucial in IDS, much like responding quickly to a security incident to minimize damage. The faster IDS detect and respond to a threat, the less harm it can cause.

IDS also serve as information gatherers, similar to investigators collecting data at a crime scene. They collect information on detected incidents, which is valuable for subsequent analysis and understanding the scope of a security breach.

Collaboration is essential in cybersecurity, much like law enforcement agencies working together to solve complex cases. IDS can share threat intelligence and insights with other security components, strengthening the overall defense against cyber threats.

Intrusion Detection Systems are like the security detail at a major event, working diligently behind the scenes to ensure the safety and security of the participants. They are an integral part of your network's defense strategy, providing real-time monitoring, threat detection, and incident response.

In summary, IDS are the vigilant guardians of your digital fortress, constantly monitoring network traffic for signs of potential threats. They detect anomalies and patterns that could indicate malicious activity, providing early warning and enabling prompt response. Collaboration and information sharing enhance their effectiveness in protecting your network. IDS are the watchful eyes that help maintain the security and integrity of your digital kingdom.

Chapter 10: Advanced Malware Analysis and Threat Intelligence

Welcome to the fascinating world of leveraging threat intelligence in malware analysis—a realm where we harness the power of knowledge and insights to dissect and understand the ever-evolving landscape of cyber threats. Think of it as equipping yourself with the latest intelligence reports and classified information to stay one step ahead of potential adversaries.

Consider threat intelligence as your secret agent, tirelessly gathering information from various sources, similar to spies collecting data on potential threats. These sources include open forums, dark web marketplaces, government agencies, and cybersecurity companies.

Threat intelligence is your early warning system, much like meteorologists predicting a storm based on weather patterns. It provides you with insights into emerging threats, enabling proactive measures to protect your digital assets.

In the world of cybersecurity, threat intelligence is like having a crystal ball that reveals the intentions of cybercriminals and the tactics they may employ. It helps you anticipate their moves and prepare your defenses accordingly.

Think of threat intelligence as a vast library of knowledge, where you can access reports, indicators of compromise (IOCs), and historical attack data. This information helps you understand the tactics, techniques, and procedures (TTPs) of threat actors.

Threat intelligence is not just about collecting data; it's about making sense of it, much like detectives analyzing clues to solve a case. Analysts dissect the information to identify patterns, trends, and potential threats.

Imagine threat intelligence as a global network of informants, each providing a piece of the puzzle. Collaboration with other organizations and sharing intelligence helps build a collective defense against cyber threats.

Threat intelligence platforms are your trusted allies, similar to personal assistants who organize and present information in a coherent manner. These platforms aggregate and analyze data, making it easier for analysts to identify relevant threats.

Consider threat intelligence feeds as daily news reports on the state of the cyber world. They provide real-time updates on emerging threats, vulnerabilities, and attacks, allowing you to stay informed and take action.

Threat intelligence analysts are like skilled investigators, examining the evidence and connecting the dots to uncover the full picture of a cyber threat. Their expertise helps you understand the motivations and goals of threat actors.

Threat intelligence is a dynamic field, much like the constantly changing nature of cyber threats. It requires continuous monitoring, analysis, and adaptation to stay effective in the ever-evolving landscape.

Think of threat intelligence as a force multiplier for your cybersecurity team. It enhances their ability to detect, respond to, and mitigate threats, making your defenses more robust and resilient.

Threat intelligence also plays a crucial role in incident response, similar to having a well-prepared emergency response plan. It helps you understand the scope of an incident, identify affected systems, and take remediation actions.

Collaboration with external threat intelligence providers is essential, much like seeking advice from experts in a specialized field. These providers offer insights and data that may not be available within your organization.

Threat intelligence is not just about defending against known threats; it also helps you anticipate and prepare for future challenges, much like a chess player thinking several moves ahead.

In summary, leveraging threat intelligence in malware analysis is like having a strategic advantage in the ever-evolving battlefield of cybersecurity. It provides you with insights, knowledge, and early warnings to defend against emerging threats. Collaboration and information sharing with other organizations enhance your collective defense. Threat intelligence is your secret weapon in the ongoing battle to protect your digital assets and stay one step ahead of cyber adversaries.

Welcome to the advanced realm of malware analysis and attribution—a domain where we delve deeper into the intricate world of cyber threats, dissecting malicious code, and uncovering the identities behind these digital adversaries. It's akin to becoming a digital detective, equipped with advanced tools and techniques to solve the mysteries of cybercrime.

Advanced malware analysis is like a forensic examination of a crime scene, where we meticulously collect evidence, scrutinize it, and reconstruct the events that led to the cyberattack. It's about understanding the "how" and "why" behind the malicious code.

Imagine malware analysis as a journey into the dark alleys of the digital world, where we follow the trail of malicious code, trying to uncover the motives and intentions of cybercriminals.

Advanced techniques in malware analysis go beyond the surface, similar to forensic experts using specialized equipment to examine trace evidence. We dig deep into the code to understand its behavior, evasion techniques, and potential impact.

Consider malware analysis as a chess game, where we anticipate the moves of our opponents—cybercriminals. We strategize to outsmart them by understanding their tactics and uncovering their digital footprints.

Attribution in malware analysis is like identifying a criminal's signature at a crime scene. It involves tracing the origin of the malware and determining who is behind it, similar to identifying a suspect in a criminal investigation.

Advanced malware analysis techniques are like using cutting-edge technology to solve complex puzzles. We employ dynamic and static analysis, reverse engineering, and code dissection to unveil the inner workings of malicious software.

Think of malware analysis as decrypting a hidden message. We dissect the code, analyze its functions, and uncover the secrets concealed within, much like codebreakers deciphering encrypted communications.

Advanced malware analysis is a continuous learning process, similar to staying updated on the latest criminal tactics and adapting our investigative methods accordingly.

Malware analysis and attribution require a deep understanding of the digital landscape, akin to studying the behavior of various criminal organizations to predict their next moves.

Consider advanced malware analysis as a collaboration between digital detectives, sharing insights and intelligence to piece together the puzzle of cyber threats.

Attribution is like finding a needle in a digital haystack. We gather clues, follow leads, and analyze patterns to identify the threat actor responsible for a cyberattack.

Advanced malware analysis also involves exploring the motivations behind cyberattacks, similar to understanding the motives of criminals in traditional investigations.

Think of malware attribution as tracking down a mastermind behind a criminal syndicate. We connect the dots, gather evidence, and build a case against the threat actor.

Advanced malware analysis goes beyond identifying the malware itself; it's about understanding the tactics, techniques, and procedures (TTPs) employed by cybercriminals.

Malware analysis is not just about identifying threats; it's about developing countermeasures to protect against future attacks, similar to improving security measures in response to criminal activities.

Attribution in malware analysis is a complex endeavor, much like untangling a web of deceit to reveal the true identities of cybercriminals.

Consider advanced malware analysis as a strategic game, where we anticipate the moves of threat actors and develop strategies to outmaneuver them.

Malware analysis and attribution require a combination of technical expertise, analytical skills, and a deep understanding of the evolving threat landscape.

In summary, advanced techniques in malware analysis and attribution are like becoming digital detectives, equipped with the knowledge and tools to uncover the secrets of cyber threats. It's about going beyond the surface and understanding the inner workings of malicious code. Attribution is like identifying the culprits behind a crime, tracing the origin of malware, and understanding the motives of threat actors. Collaboration and continuous learning are essential in this ever-evolving field, as we work together to stay one step ahead of cyber adversaries. Advanced malware analysis is the key to protecting our digital world from evolving threats and ensuring a safer online environment.

BOOK 3
ADVANCED CYBERSECURITY THREAT ANALYSIS AND INCIDENT RESPONSE

ROB BOTWRIGHT

Chapter 1: The Evolving Threat Landscape

Let's embark on a journey through the historical context of cyber threats—a fascinating exploration that takes us from the early days of computing to the complex, interconnected world of today. Think of it as tracing the evolution of digital adversaries and their tactics over time, much like studying the history of warfare to understand modern conflict.

Imagine a world where computers were massive, room-filling machines, and the concept of cyber threats was in its infancy. It was the 1960s, and the digital landscape was vastly different from what we know today. There were no viruses or malware as we understand them, but there were the seeds of what would become cyber threats.

In the 1970s, the birth of personal computers brought about new possibilities and vulnerabilities. The first viruses emerged, created not with malicious intent but as experiments. These early viruses were like the pioneers of cyber threats, exploring the digital frontier.

As we entered the 1980s, the landscape began to shift. The Morris Worm, unleashed in 1988, marked a significant milestone in cyber threats. It was one of the first instances of malicious code spreading rapidly across the internet, highlighting the potential for widespread digital disruption.

In the 1990s, cyber threats took a more organized form with the emergence of hacking groups. It was a decade marked by high-profile incidents like the hacking of

NASA and the Pentagon. The digital realm was becoming a battleground, and the motivations behind cyberattacks were evolving.

The early 2000s witnessed the rise of financially motivated cybercrime. Malware like the Code Red and Slammer worms disrupted networks worldwide, causing financial losses and highlighting the profit potential of cyber threats.

The mid-2000s brought the era of state-sponsored cyberattacks into the spotlight. Nations began using cyber espionage and cyber warfare tactics, blurring the lines between cyber threats and national security concerns. Stuxnet, a sophisticated malware targeting Iran's nuclear program, exemplified the power of state-sponsored cyberattacks.

As we moved further into the 21st century, cyber threats continued to evolve. Ransomware became a prevalent threat, with attackers encrypting data and demanding ransom payments. It was like a digital version of hostage-taking, where victims had to pay to regain access to their own data.

The 2010s saw a surge in data breaches, with cybercriminals targeting organizations to steal sensitive information. Large-scale breaches, such as the one at Equifax, exposed the vulnerabilities of our digital infrastructure.

The proliferation of the internet of things (IoT) brought new challenges. Devices from smart refrigerators to industrial control systems became potential targets for cyberattacks, expanding the attack surface for cyber threats.

Today, the digital landscape is more complex than ever. Cyber threats have evolved into a global industry, with cybercriminals, hacktivists, nation-states, and even insiders participating in the cyber battlefield. Attacks range from sophisticated nation-state operations to relatively simple but effective phishing scams.

The motivations behind cyber threats vary widely, from financial gain to political agendas and even ideological beliefs. Some cybercriminals seek financial rewards, while others aim to disrupt critical infrastructure or steal sensitive information. Understanding these motivations is crucial to combating cyber threats effectively.

The tools and tactics of cyber threats continue to advance, with malware becoming increasingly sophisticated and evasive. Threat actors are skilled at bypassing traditional security measures, making it challenging to defend against their attacks.

In summary, the historical context of cyber threats is a journey through the evolution of digital adversaries, from the early days of computing to the complex landscape of today. It's a story of how technology has enabled new forms of threats and how motivations behind cyberattacks have evolved. As we navigate this ever-changing landscape, understanding the past is essential to prepare for the challenges of the future and ensure a safer digital world for all.

Let's dive into the dynamic world of the current threat landscape—a constantly evolving ecosystem of digital risks and challenges. Think of it as a journey through the ever-shifting sands of cyber threats, where we explore the latest trends and patterns in the world of cybersecurity.

Picture a landscape where cyber threats are not static but in a perpetual state of flux. It's akin to observing the changing seasons, where new threats emerge, and old ones adapt to survive. Understanding these trends is essential in navigating the digital terrain.

In this ever-evolving threat landscape, one of the prominent trends is the proliferation of ransomware attacks. These attacks have become more targeted and sophisticated, with cybercriminals demanding hefty ransoms to decrypt valuable data. It's like a modern-day form of digital extortion.

Another notable trend is the rise of supply chain attacks. Cybercriminals are no longer targeting just individual organizations but are infiltrating the software and hardware supply chain. This allows them to compromise multiple entities simultaneously, creating a ripple effect of cyber disruption.

Consider the threat landscape as a vast ocean where phishing attacks are the relentless waves. Phishing has evolved into a highly effective method for attackers to deceive individuals and organizations, often using social engineering techniques to lure victims into clicking malicious links or sharing sensitive information.

Cryptocurrency-related threats have also gained prominence. With the proliferation of cryptocurrencies, cybercriminals have found new ways to profit. Cryptomining malware and cryptojacking attacks have become common, hijacking victims' devices to mine digital currencies.

The Internet of Things (IoT) has added a new dimension to the threat landscape. IoT devices, from smart thermostats to connected cameras, often lack robust security measures, making them attractive targets for attackers. It's like having multiple entry points into a digital fortress.

Nation-state cyberattacks continue to be a significant concern. State-sponsored threat actors engage in espionage, cyber warfare, and information warfare. These attacks blur the line between traditional espionage and digital conflict, posing challenges for attribution and international relations.

Think of the threat landscape as a digital bazaar, where cybercriminals offer a range of malicious services for sale on the dark web. These services include exploit kits, malware-as-a-service, and stolen data markets, allowing even novice attackers to access advanced tools.

The use of artificial intelligence (AI) and machine learning (ML) is another trend in the threat landscape. Attackers leverage AI to automate tasks like reconnaissance and evasion, while defenders use AI for threat detection and response, creating a digital arms race.

Consider the threat landscape as a vast ecosystem where threat intelligence plays a vital role. Organizations and cybersecurity professionals rely on threat intelligence feeds and platforms to stay informed about emerging threats and vulnerabilities.

Cloud security is a growing concern as organizations increasingly migrate their data and services to the cloud. While cloud providers offer robust security measures, misconfigured cloud environments can expose sensitive data to the internet, making it a target for attackers.

In this ever-changing landscape, zero-day vulnerabilities pose a significant threat. These are unknown vulnerabilities in software or hardware that attackers can exploit before vendors release patches. It's like navigating a maze where new traps appear unexpectedly.

The human element remains a critical factor in the threat landscape. Social engineering attacks, such as spear-phishing and business email compromise, target individuals' trust and behavior, making cybersecurity awareness and training essential.

Imagine the threat landscape as a global chessboard where threat actors move their pieces strategically. Cyberattacks can be part of broader geopolitical conflicts or economic rivalries, and understanding the geopolitical context is crucial.

The threat landscape is not limited to the digital realm but extends to the physical world through cyber-physical attacks. These attacks target critical infrastructure, such as power grids and transportation systems, highlighting the need for comprehensive cybersecurity measures.

In summary, the current trends in the threat landscape paint a dynamic picture of the digital risks and challenges organizations and individuals face today. It's an ever-evolving ecosystem where cyber threats take on new forms and tactics. Navigating this landscape requires vigilance, adaptability, and a proactive approach to cybersecurity. Understanding these trends is the first step in building effective defenses and ensuring a safer digital future for all.

Chapter 2: Advanced Threat Actors and Techniques

Let's embark on a journey into the intriguing world of nation-state actors and Advanced Persistent Threats (APTs). Think of it as uncovering the hidden layers of international cyber espionage, where governments and their clandestine cyber units engage in a digital game of chess.

Imagine a world where the lines between traditional espionage and cyber operations blur. In this realm, nation-state actors are the central players, wielding the power of their resources and expertise to achieve political, economic, and military objectives through cyberspace.

Picture nation-state actors as skilled spies of the digital age, operating with a level of sophistication that rivals their real-world counterparts. These state-sponsored cyber units are not bound by borders, and they operate in the shadows, often beyond the reach of conventional law enforcement.

Consider APTs as the elite forces of nation-state actors. These groups are not interested in quick hits or financial gain but focus on long-term, strategic objectives. They are like digital special forces, meticulously planning and executing cyber operations over extended periods.

In this world of nation-state actors and APTs, attribution becomes a complex puzzle. Cyberattacks are often designed to be stealthy and deniable, making it challenging to definitively identify the culprits. It's like investigating a crime where the suspects wear masks and leave no fingerprints.

Think of nation-state actors as having a vast toolkit at their disposal. They employ a wide range of tactics, techniques, and procedures (TTPs) to achieve their goals. These tools may include custom malware, zero-day vulnerabilities, and advanced social engineering.

Consider APTs as patient and persistent adversaries. They are willing to invest time and resources in their operations, often conducting extensive reconnaissance before launching an attack. It's like a chess player studying the board for hours before making a move.

In this landscape, nation-state actors often focus on specific targets of strategic importance. These targets could be government agencies, critical infrastructure, defense contractors, or research institutions. It's like espionage agents infiltrating key institutions to gather intelligence.

Imagine APTs as adept infiltrators, using spear-phishing and watering hole attacks to breach their targets' defenses. Once inside, they move stealthily, avoiding detection and quietly exfiltrating valuable information. It's like a skilled cat burglar navigating a laser-guarded vault.

Consider the motivations behind these cyber operations. Nation-state actors may seek to steal intellectual property, gain insights into their adversaries' military capabilities, or disrupt critical infrastructure. It's like the digital equivalent of espionage, sabotage, and reconnaissance.

In this world, the private sector is not immune to nation-state actors and APTs. Corporations and businesses are often caught in the crossfire, either as unwitting victims or as targets themselves. It's like collateral damage in a cyber conflict.

Imagine the role of cybersecurity experts and threat analysts. They act as digital detectives, piecing together clues, analyzing malware samples, and tracing the footprints of nation-state actors. It's like solving a complex puzzle with global implications.

Consider the international dimension of these cyber operations. Nation-state actors often operate on a global scale, with targets and victims spanning multiple countries. It's like a geopolitical chessboard where moves in cyberspace have real-world consequences.

In this landscape, the cat-and-mouse game between defenders and nation-state actors is ongoing. Cybersecurity professionals constantly adapt their defenses, share threat intelligence, and collaborate with law enforcement to counter APTs. It's like a high-stakes game of chess, where every move counts.

Imagine the importance of international norms and agreements in this realm. Governments and organizations work together to establish rules of behavior in cyberspace, deter malicious actors, and hold them accountable for their actions. It's like crafting a treaty to prevent cyber conflict.

Consider the evolving nature of nation-state cyber capabilities. As technology advances, so do the tools and techniques available to APTs. Cyber arms races and espionage in the digital age are ongoing battles of innovation and adaptation.

In this world, the challenge of defending against nation-state actors and APTs is ever-present. Organizations must invest in robust cybersecurity measures, employee training, and incident response capabilities. It's like fortifying a fortress to withstand relentless attacks.

In summary, nation-state actors and APTs represent a complex and dynamic landscape in the world of cybersecurity. They are the digital spies and covert operatives of our time, engaging in a silent but high-stakes battle for information and influence. Understanding their tactics and motivations is essential for governments, organizations, and individuals to protect themselves in an interconnected and vulnerable world.

Welcome to the fascinating realm of advanced attack techniques and tactics. In this chapter, we'll delve deep into the sophisticated methods employed by cyber adversaries to breach systems, steal data, and achieve their malicious objectives.

Imagine cyber attackers as skilled craftsmen, continually refining their techniques to exploit vulnerabilities and evade detection. They operate in a dynamic environment where innovation is the norm, much like artisans perfecting their craft.

Picture the cyber threat landscape as a vast canvas, and attack techniques as the brush strokes that create intricate and sometimes destructive digital masterpieces. These techniques are not static but evolve over time, adapting to changing technologies and defenses.

Consider the concept of "zero-day vulnerabilities." These are flaws in software or hardware that are unknown to the vendor and, therefore, unpatched. Attackers covet these vulnerabilities, using them as secret weapons to infiltrate systems undetected.

Think of social engineering as the art of persuasion in the digital age. Attackers employ psychological manipulation to trick individuals into revealing sensitive information or performing actions that compromise security. It's akin to a digital con game.

Consider the "watering hole" attack technique. Attackers identify websites frequented by their target audience and compromise those sites with malware. When unsuspecting visitors land on these compromised pages, they become unwitting victims. It's like setting a trap in the digital wilderness.

Imagine the use of "spear-phishing" attacks. Unlike generic phishing attempts, spear-phishing is highly targeted. Attackers research their victims, crafting convincing and personalized messages to increase the chances of success. It's like tailoring a suit for a specific individual.

Picture the concept of "fileless malware." Traditional malware relies on files stored on a system, making it detectable. Fileless malware operates in memory, leaving no traces on the disk. It's like a ghostly presence in the digital realm, hard to spot and harder to eradicate.

Consider the use of "living off the land" tactics. Attackers leverage legitimate tools and utilities already present on a system to carry out their malicious activities. This technique allows them to blend in with normal user behavior, making detection challenging.

Think of "advanced evasion techniques" used by attackers to avoid detection by security solutions. These techniques involve manipulating the network traffic or the behavior of malware to slip past security measures, much like a skilled magician diverting attention.

Imagine the concept of "island hopping." Attackers target not only the primary victim but also organizations connected to them through supply chains or partnerships. By compromising one entity, they gain a foothold to access others. It's like a digital chain reaction.

Consider the use of "exfiltration techniques." Once attackers gain access to a network, they must extract valuable data. They employ various methods to do so, often encrypting and disguising the stolen information to avoid detection during the exfiltration process.

Picture the "living-off-the-land" approach in lateral movement. Attackers move laterally within a compromised network, hopping from one system to another using legitimate administrative tools, making it challenging for defenders to distinguish malicious from legitimate actions.

Think of "steganography" as the art of hiding in plain sight. Attackers conceal data within images, audio files, or other seemingly harmless files, making it virtually impossible to detect without specialized tools. It's like a secret message hidden within a painting.

Consider the use of "malware-as-a-service" offerings on the dark web. Cybercriminals can rent or purchase malware and hacking tools, lowering the bar for entry into the world of cybercrime. It's like a digital black market where malicious services are readily available.

Imagine the "fileless persistence" techniques employed by attackers to maintain access to a compromised system. They manipulate registry settings, scheduled tasks, or other system components, ensuring that their presence persists even after a reboot.

Think of "living off the land" in data exfiltration. Attackers often use legitimate network protocols and channels to sneak stolen data out of a network, making it appear as routine traffic and evading detection.

Consider the concept of "tunneling" to evade network security measures. Attackers encapsulate their malicious traffic within encrypted tunnels, making it appear as normal encrypted traffic, which is challenging to inspect.

Picture the use of "anti-forensic techniques." After a successful attack, attackers may attempt to erase their tracks, manipulate logs, or otherwise obfuscate their actions to hinder post-incident investigation.

Imagine the use of "supply chain attacks" to compromise trusted software or hardware vendors. Attackers infiltrate the supply chain to infect software updates or hardware components, which then get distributed to unsuspecting customers, amplifying the impact of their attack.

Consider the "isolation and persistence" tactics employed by attackers. They isolate compromised systems from the network to prevent detection while maintaining persistence through covert channels, ensuring ongoing access.

Think of the "living-off-the-land" approach in obfuscation. Attackers may employ legitimate coding practices and tools to make their malicious code appear benign to security solutions.

Picture "deepfake" technology, which allows attackers to create convincing audio and video content that impersonates individuals. These deepfakes can be used for various malicious purposes, from disinformation campaigns to fraud.

Consider the use of "fileless privilege escalation" techniques. Attackers seek vulnerabilities in operating systems or software to elevate their privileges within a compromised system, granting them greater control and access.

Imagine the "island hopping" strategy extending to cloud services. Attackers target cloud service providers or their clients to gain access to valuable data stored in the cloud, expanding the scope of their attacks.

Think of "counter-incident response" tactics used by attackers to thwart defenders' efforts. They may actively monitor and counteract incident response actions, hindering the investigation and containment of their activities.

Consider the use of "custom malware frameworks" developed by advanced threat actors. These frameworks provide attackers with a modular and adaptable toolkit for carrying out their operations.

Picture the challenge of attribution in the world of advanced attack techniques. Attackers often employ false flags and deception techniques to mislead investigators and obscure their true identities.

In this ever-evolving landscape of advanced attack techniques and tactics, defenders must remain vigilant, adaptive, and proactive. Understanding the intricacies of these techniques is crucial for building robust defenses and staying one step ahead of cyber adversaries.

Chapter 3: Threat Intelligence Gathering

Let's explore the rich and dynamic world of threat intelligence, a critical component in the ongoing battle against cyber threats.

Threat intelligence is like a puzzle, with pieces scattered across the digital landscape. These pieces come from a variety of sources, each contributing valuable insights.

One key source of threat intelligence is the "open-source community." Imagine it as a global network of digital detectives, constantly scouring the internet for traces of malicious activity. They share their findings freely, contributing to the collective knowledge base.

Consider the "security blogs and forums" as treasure troves of insights. Cybersecurity experts and enthusiasts share their experiences, analyses, and discoveries in these online spaces. It's like a vibrant marketplace of ideas where information flows freely.

Picture "vulnerability databases" as reference libraries for security researchers. They catalog known software vulnerabilities, providing a valuable resource for defenders seeking to patch weaknesses before attackers can exploit them.

Think of "dark web monitoring" as a digital undercover operation. Researchers infiltrate hidden corners of the internet frequented by cybercriminals, gathering intelligence on upcoming threats and illicit activities.

Consider "honeypots and decoys" as digital bait. Security professionals set up these virtual traps to lure in attackers and observe their tactics, techniques, and procedures. It's like studying wildlife in their natural habitat.

Imagine the "security research organizations" as vigilant guardians. They dedicate themselves to tracking emerging threats and sharing their findings with the wider community, helping others stay informed and protected.

Think of "government agencies" as sentinels on the cyber frontier. They have a broader perspective and access to classified information, which can provide critical threat intelligence. It's like having a watchtower with a view of the entire landscape.

Consider "information sharing and analysis centers (ISACs)" as hubs of collaboration. Organizations in various industries come together to pool their threat intelligence, fostering a stronger collective defense against common adversaries.

Picture "commercial threat intelligence providers" as specialized guides. They offer tailored intelligence feeds and reports to organizations, helping them navigate the complex threat landscape.

Think of "incident response teams" as first responders to cyber threats. They gather valuable intelligence during their investigations, which can then be shared with the broader community to enhance collective defense.

Consider "cybersecurity vendors" as guardians of their customers' digital realms. They collect intelligence from their extensive customer base and use it to develop better security products and services.

Imagine the power of "machine learning and artificial intelligence" in threat intelligence. These technologies can sift through vast amounts of data, identifying patterns and anomalies that human analysts might miss. Think of "academic institutions" as research pioneers. They conduct in-depth studies on emerging threats and vulnerabilities, contributing to our understanding of the evolving threat landscape.

Consider "social media and online communities" as digital watering holes. Attackers often discuss their activities in these spaces, leaving digital footprints that can be analyzed for threat intelligence.

Picture "threat feeds" as constantly flowing rivers of data. These streams provide real-time information on known threats, enabling organizations to block or mitigate them swiftly.

Think of "cybersecurity conferences" as annual gatherings of the brightest minds in the field. Experts share their research and insights, advancing our collective understanding of cyber threats.

Imagine "collaborative threat-sharing platforms" as bridges between organizations. They facilitate the exchange of threat intelligence in a secure and standardized manner.

Consider the "cybersecurity industry's own experiences" as a wellspring of knowledge. Lessons learned from past incidents and breaches inform future defenses, creating a feedback loop of intelligence.

Picture "global incident response networks" as a worldwide web of cybersecurity defenders. They coordinate responses to large-scale threats, sharing intelligence and strategies to contain and mitigate attacks.

Think of "regulatory bodies and compliance requirements" as drivers of better threat intelligence practices. Compliance mandates often include reporting and information-sharing requirements to enhance collective security.

Imagine "cyber threat research reports" as guidebooks through the ever-changing landscape. These reports provide comprehensive analyses of threats, helping organizations understand the risks they face.

Consider "cybersecurity partnerships" as alliances forged in the fires of shared challenges. Organizations come together to pool their resources and intelligence, strengthening their defenses.

Picture "cyber threat intelligence platforms" as command centers. They aggregate, analyze, and visualize threat data, providing organizations with actionable intelligence to make informed decisions.

Think of "security information and event management (SIEM) systems" as watchful sentinels. They collect and correlate data from various sources to detect and alert on potential threats in real-time.

Consider "collaborative threat-hunting teams" as detectives on the digital beat. They proactively seek out threats within their organizations, uncovering hidden dangers before they can wreak havoc.

Imagine "cybersecurity training and awareness programs" as empowering individuals. Educated employees are more likely to recognize and report potential threats, adding a human layer to threat intelligence.

Think of "cyber threat intelligence sharing platforms" as information marketplaces. Organizations can exchange threat data, enriching their own intelligence while helping others.

Consider "industry-specific threat intelligence" as tailored insights. Different sectors face unique threats, and specialized threat intelligence can help organizations in those sectors stay vigilant.

Picture "cross-sector collaboration" as a force multiplier. When organizations across industries come together to share threat intelligence, the entire ecosystem becomes more resilient.

Think of "legal and regulatory frameworks for threat intelligence sharing" as enablers of cooperation. These frameworks provide guidelines and protections for organizations that share intelligence.

Imagine "ethical hacking and bug bounty programs" as two-way streets. White-hat hackers discover vulnerabilities and report them to organizations, contributing to threat intelligence.

Consider "red teaming and penetration testing" as simulated attacks. These exercises help organizations identify weaknesses in their defenses and contribute to a better understanding of potential threats.

Picture "threat intelligence feeds" as streams of awareness. These feeds provide real-time updates on emerging threats, ensuring organizations are informed and prepared.

Think of "international cooperation in threat intelligence sharing" as a united front. Cyber threats know no borders, and collaboration between nations can be instrumental in countering them.

Imagine "community-driven threat intelligence" as the wisdom of crowds. A collective effort to share insights and experiences can enhance the overall understanding of the threat landscape.

Consider "threat intelligence platforms with automation" as force multipliers. Automated processes can rapidly analyze and distribute threat intelligence, enabling quicker responses.

Picture "dark web monitoring and analysis" as peering into the shadows. Understanding the activities of cybercriminals in hidden corners of the internet can yield valuable threat intelligence.

Think of "threat intelligence fusion centers" as hubs of integration. They consolidate information from various sources, providing a comprehensive view of the threat landscape.

Imagine "continuous threat intelligence sharing" as an ongoing dialogue. In the ever-evolving world of cyber threats, constant communication is key to staying ahead.

Consider "strategic threat intelligence partnerships" as alliances for the long haul. Collaborations that endure over time can yield deeper insights and better defense strategies.

Picture "automated threat intelligence sharing platforms" as swift messengers. These platforms ensure that threat intelligence reaches the right people at the right time, reducing response times.

Think of "threat intelligence analysis tools" as magnifying glasses for data. They help analysts sift through vast amounts of information to extract actionable intelligence.

Consider "publicly available threat feeds" as open-source intelligence. These feeds are accessible to anyone and can serve as valuable sources of threat information.

Imagine "threat intelligence training programs" as schools for defenders. Training equips individuals with the skills to effectively gather, analyze, and use threat intelligence.

Think of "government-industry partnerships" as collaborations with a broader reach. When governments work with private sector organizations, threat intelligence sharing becomes more comprehensive.

Consider "global threat intelligence communities" as vast networks of collaboration. In an interconnected world, these communities help organizations stay informed and protected.

Picture "intelligence-led security strategies" as blueprints for defense. By incorporating threat intelligence into their strategies, organizations can build more resilient security postures.

In the world of cybersecurity, knowledge is power, and threat intelligence is the fuel that propels defenders forward. By harnessing insights from diverse sources, organizations can better understand, anticipate, and counter the ever-evolving landscape of cyber threats.

Let's delve into the world of threat intelligence, exploring how it's not just about collecting data but also about turning that information into actionable insights that can bolster your cybersecurity defenses.

At its core, threat intelligence is like the weather forecast for the digital world, providing you with critical information about potential storms and sunny days in the cyber landscape.

Imagine threat intelligence as a vast puzzle, with pieces scattered across the digital realm, and your job is to put those pieces together to see the bigger picture.

Think of it as the digital equivalent of having a network of informants who provide you with timely information about the activities of cybercriminals, giving you a heads-up on their plans and tactics.

Threat intelligence is your early warning system, alerting you to potential threats before they become full-blown attacks, allowing you to prepare and respond effectively.

Consider it as a crystal ball that helps you foresee emerging threats, vulnerabilities, and trends in the cyber world, allowing you to stay one step ahead of cyber adversaries.

It's like having a digital detective on your team, constantly gathering clues and evidence from various sources to uncover the mysteries of the cyber landscape.

Think of threat intelligence as your cyber compass, guiding you through the ever-changing terrain of cyber threats, helping you navigate safely.

Imagine it as a guardian angel for your digital assets, tirelessly monitoring the digital realm and warning you of impending danger.

Picture threat intelligence as a flashlight in the dark corners of the internet, revealing hidden threats and vulnerabilities that would otherwise go unnoticed.

Think of it as the storyteller of the cyber world, weaving narratives from disparate pieces of data, helping you understand the motives and tactics of cybercriminals.

Consider it as a force multiplier for your cybersecurity team, empowering them with the knowledge and insights needed to defend your organization effectively.

Imagine threat intelligence as a treasure map, leading you to the vulnerabilities and weaknesses that attackers might exploit, allowing you to fortify your defenses.

Think of it as a crystal-clear mirror, reflecting the true state of your organization's cybersecurity posture, helping you identify areas that need improvement.

Picture threat intelligence as a strategic advisor, offering recommendations on how to allocate resources and prioritize security efforts based on the most significant threats.

Consider it as a guardian of your digital reputation, helping you proactively protect your brand and customer trust by preventing data breaches and cyber incidents.

Imagine threat intelligence as a map of the cyber battlefield, showing you where the enemy is lurking and how they might attack, enabling you to strategize your defense.

Think of it as a radar system for your digital assets, constantly scanning the horizon for incoming threats and raising the alarm when danger is detected.

Picture threat intelligence as a global network of cyber allies, where organizations come together to share insights and collaborate in the fight against cybercrime.

Consider it as a microscope that allows you to zoom in on specific threats, dissecting them to understand their inner workings and vulnerabilities.

Imagine threat intelligence as a shield that protects your organization from cyberattacks, providing you with the information needed to fortify your defenses.

Think of it as a crystal ball that helps you anticipate the moves of cyber adversaries, enabling you to stay ahead in the ever-evolving game of cybersecurity.

Picture threat intelligence as a digital librarian, categorizing and organizing vast amounts of data into meaningful information that can be used to make informed decisions.

Consider it as a detective's magnifying glass, helping you uncover hidden clues and patterns in the vast sea of digital information.

Imagine threat intelligence as a guardian at the gates of your organization, ensuring that only the good traffic gets through while blocking the bad actors.

Think of it as a lighthouse that guides you through the stormy seas of cyberspace, helping you avoid the treacherous rocks of cyber threats.

Picture threat intelligence as a compass that points you in the right direction, helping you make decisions that will keep your organization safe in the digital world.

Consider it as a trusted advisor that provides you with insights and recommendations based on real-time data, helping you make the best cybersecurity decisions.

Imagine threat intelligence as a map that shows you the terrain of the digital landscape, helping you navigate the complex world of cyber threats.

Think of it as a guardian angel that watches over your digital assets, ensuring that they remain safe and secure in the face of ever-present cyber dangers.

Picture threat intelligence as a crystal ball that allows you to peer into the future of cybersecurity, giving you the foresight to prepare for what lies ahead.

Consider it as a digital detective that sifts through the noise of the internet to uncover the truth about cyber threats, allowing you to respond effectively.

Imagine threat intelligence as a shield that protects your organization from the ever-present danger of cyberattacks, helping you stay one step ahead of cybercriminals.

Think of it as a trusted advisor that provides you with insights and recommendations to strengthen your cybersecurity defenses and protect your digital assets.

Picture threat intelligence as a vigilant sentry that stands guard over your organization, keeping watch for any signs of impending cyber threats.

Consider it as a strategic ally that helps you make informed decisions and take proactive steps to safeguard your organization's digital future.

In essence, threat intelligence is your digital ally in the ongoing battle against cyber threats, providing you with the knowledge and insights needed to protect your organization and stay ahead of cybercriminals.

Chapter 4: Cybersecurity Incident Response Frameworks

Let's explore the world of incident response frameworks, which are like well-structured roadmaps that guide organizations through the chaotic and often stressful process of managing and mitigating cybersecurity incidents.

Imagine incident response frameworks as lifelines in the world of cybersecurity, providing organizations with a systematic approach to dealing with cyber threats and attacks.

Think of them as the emergency plans that organizations rely on when the digital storm clouds gather, helping them respond swiftly and effectively to protect their assets.

Consider incident response frameworks as the battle strategies that cybersecurity teams use to defend their digital territories, ensuring that they are well-prepared for any cyber skirmish.

Picture them as the safety nets that organizations have in place to catch them when they stumble into the unpredictable world of cyber incidents, preventing potential disasters.

Think of incident response frameworks as the compasses that guide organizations through the turbulent seas of cyber threats, helping them navigate uncharted waters.

Imagine them as the playbooks that cybersecurity professionals consult when the cyber alarm bells ring, ensuring that they know exactly what steps to take.

Consider incident response frameworks as the orchestration tools that coordinate the efforts of different teams within an organization, ensuring a harmonious response to cyber incidents.

Picture them as the blueprints for incident management, providing a structured approach to identifying, containing, eradicating, and recovering from cyber threats.

Think of incident response frameworks as the GPS that helps organizations find their way back to safety when they've veered off course due to a cyber incident.

Imagine them as the first-aid kits that organizations use to treat the wounds inflicted by cyberattacks, helping them heal and recover quickly.

Consider incident response frameworks as the Swiss army knives of cybersecurity, equipped with a multitude of tools and techniques to handle various types of incidents.

Picture them as the strategic guides that organizations rely on to make critical decisions during cyber crises, ensuring that they respond effectively.

Think of incident response frameworks as the referees in the cybersecurity game, ensuring that the rules are followed and that fair play prevails during incident handling.

Imagine them as the architects of resilience, helping organizations build a solid foundation for cybersecurity and ensuring that they can bounce back from incidents.

Consider incident response frameworks as the firefighters of the digital world, rushing in to extinguish the flames of cyber threats and prevent them from spreading.

Picture them as the detectives who investigate cyber incidents, gathering evidence and uncovering the who, what, when, where, and how of the attack.

Think of incident response frameworks as the crisis managers who coordinate the response efforts, ensuring that everyone is on the same page and working toward a common goal.

Imagine them as the communication hubs that keep all stakeholders informed during a cyber incident, maintaining transparency and trust.

Consider incident response frameworks as the bridges that connect cybersecurity with the broader organizational strategy, ensuring that incident response aligns with business goals.

Picture them as the trainers who prepare cybersecurity teams for the unexpected, conducting drills and exercises to sharpen their skills.

Think of incident response frameworks as the troubleshooters who diagnose the root causes of cyber incidents, preventing recurrence in the future.

Imagine them as the architects of resilience, helping organizations build robust cybersecurity postures that can withstand the test of time.

Consider incident response frameworks as the guardians of data and assets, ensuring that organizations protect what matters most during cyber incidents.

Picture them as the negotiators who may engage with cybercriminals during ransomware incidents, seeking to resolve the situation without further harm.

Think of incident response frameworks as the educators who raise awareness within organizations, ensuring that employees understand their role in incident response.

Imagine them as the community builders who foster collaboration and knowledge sharing among cybersecurity professionals, strengthening the collective defense against cyber threats.

Consider incident response frameworks as the compasses that guide organizations through the ever-evolving landscape of cyber threats, helping them stay on course.

Picture them as the safety nets that organizations rely on to catch them when they stumble into the unpredictable world of cyber incidents, preventing potential disasters.

In essence, incident response frameworks are the trusted companions that organizations turn to when the unexpected happens in the digital realm, providing guidance, structure, and expertise to help them weather the storm of cyber incidents and emerge stronger on the other side. Next, let's dive into the essential aspects of implementing an incident response plan, which is like having a well-rehearsed emergency protocol for your organization's cybersecurity.

Imagine your incident response plan as the safety net that you've diligently set up to catch any unexpected cyber incidents, ensuring that your organization can bounce back swiftly and effectively.

Think of it as your organization's proactive approach to handling the digital storms that may come your way, much like having a storm shelter prepared for a tornado. Consider your incident response plan as the conductor's baton in a cybersecurity orchestra, harmonizing the efforts of various teams to respond efficiently to incidents. Picture it as the trusted guide that leads your organization through the maze of cyber threats, making sure you navigate the complex landscape with confidence.

Think of your incident response plan as the crisis manager's playbook, detailing the steps to take when cyber chaos erupts, helping you maintain order and control. Imagine it as the map that shows you the path to follow when cyber danger lurks, helping you avoid pitfalls and reach the safety of cybersecurity resilience.

Consider your incident response plan as the compass that points you in the right direction, ensuring that your organization stays on course during the turbulent times of cyber incidents.

Picture it as the communication hub that keeps everyone informed, ensuring that your organization's response is coordinated, transparent, and effective.

Think of your incident response plan as the firefighter's toolkit for the digital world, equipped with strategies and tactics to extinguish cyber threats and prevent them from spreading.

Imagine it as the detective's magnifying glass, helping you uncover the clues and evidence needed to understand the nature and origin of the cyber incident.

Consider your incident response plan as the guardian of your organization's data and reputation, ensuring that you protect what matters most during an incident.

Picture it as the bridge that connects your cybersecurity team with other departments, aligning incident response efforts with the broader organizational strategy.

Think of your incident response plan as the crisis negotiator, ready to engage with cybercriminals during ransomware incidents, seeking to resolve the situation with minimal harm.

Imagine it as the educator that raises awareness within your organization, ensuring that employees understand their roles in incident response and cybersecurity.

Consider your incident response plan as the proactive trainer, conducting drills and exercises to prepare your team for the unexpected, making sure they are well-equipped.

Picture it as the troubleshooter who identifies the root causes of cyber incidents, preventing their recurrence and improving your organization's overall security posture.

Think of your incident response plan as the resilient foundation upon which your organization can weather the storm of cyber threats and emerge stronger.

Imagine it as the guardian that maintains your organization's reputation and customer trust, even in the face of cyber incidents.

Consider your incident response plan as the crisis communicator, conveying the right messages to stakeholders, clients, and the public, maintaining trust and credibility.

Picture it as the community builder, fostering collaboration and knowledge sharing among cybersecurity professionals, strengthening your collective defense against cyber threats.

Think of your incident response plan as the adaptable playbook, capable of evolving to address new and emerging cyber threats in a rapidly changing digital landscape.

Imagine it as the compass that guides your organization through the ever-shifting terrain of cybersecurity, ensuring that you stay on the right path.

Consider your incident response plan as the proactive guardian of your digital assets, ready to defend them at a moment's notice and mitigate the impact of any incident.

Picture it as the strategic ally, offering insights and recommendations to improve your cybersecurity posture and protect your organization from future threats.

Think of your incident response plan as the proactive companion on your cybersecurity journey, always ready to help you navigate the unpredictable waters of cyber incidents with confidence and resilience.

In essence, implementing an incident response plan is like having a trusted partner by your side, ready to assist you in times of cyber crisis and ensuring that your organization emerges from incidents stronger and more prepared for the future.

Chapter 5: Incident Identification and Triage

Now, let's delve into the important world of detecting and classifying security incidents, a crucial aspect of maintaining a resilient cybersecurity posture.

Think of detecting and classifying security incidents as akin to having a watchful guardian for your digital kingdom, constantly on the lookout for signs of trouble and ready to spring into action when needed.

Consider it as your organization's vigilant sentinel, equipped with the ability to identify and categorize potential threats before they escalate into full-blown incidents.

Picture it as the early-warning system that can alert your cybersecurity team to even the subtlest hints of suspicious activity, allowing for proactive response.

Think of detecting and classifying security incidents as your organization's digital detective, skilled at recognizing patterns and anomalies that might indicate a breach.

Imagine it as the radar system that scans your network for any unusual blips or irregularities, serving as a digital security guard.

Consider it as the gatekeeper that screens incoming and outgoing data, looking for any signs of unauthorized access or data exfiltration.

Think of detecting and classifying security incidents as the gatekeeper that screens incoming and outgoing data, looking for any signs of unauthorized access or data exfiltration.

Picture it as the traffic cop of your digital infrastructure, directing and monitoring the flow of data to ensure safe and secure operations.

Think of detecting and classifying security incidents as the digital sleuth that carefully examines logs, files, and network traffic for any clues of malicious intent.

Imagine it as the digital microscope that zooms in on the smallest details, seeking out the proverbial needles in the haystack of data.

Consider it as the cybersecurity expert who knows the ins and outs of various threat indicators, ready to recognize and categorize them.

Think of detecting and classifying security incidents as the guardian of your organization's digital assets, ensuring that threats are identified and assessed promptly.

Imagine it as the digital librarian that catalogs and organizes security-related events, making it easier for your cybersecurity team to respond effectively.

Consider it as the translator that deciphers the language of cyber threats, turning cryptic data into actionable insights.

Think of detecting and classifying security incidents as the cybersecurity analyst's trusted companion, helping them make sense of the complex threat landscape.

Imagine it as the digital consultant that offers recommendations for mitigating the impact of security incidents based on their classification.

Consider it as the digital historian that maintains a record of past incidents, enabling your organization to learn from previous experiences.

Think of detecting and classifying security incidents as the guardian of your organization's reputation, ensuring that any breaches or intrusions are identified and handled with care.

Imagine it as the alarm system that sounds the alert when something unusual occurs, prompting a rapid and well-coordinated response.

Consider it as the digital archaeologist that excavates the details of a security incident, piecing together the story of what happened.

Think of detecting and classifying security incidents as the early responder, minimizing the damage and fallout that can result from a cyberattack.

Imagine it as the digital psychologist that delves into the motivations and tactics of threat actors, helping your organization understand the nature of the threat.

Consider it as the digital triage nurse that assesses the severity of a security incident, ensuring that the most critical issues receive immediate attention.

Think of detecting and classifying security incidents as the cybersecurity team's trusted sidekick, working alongside them to protect your organization's digital assets.

Imagine it as the digital weather vane that detects the shifting winds of cyber threats, allowing your organization to adjust its defenses accordingly.

Consider it as the digital mentor that guides your cybersecurity team in their efforts to safeguard your organization from harm.

Think of detecting and classifying security incidents as the guardian of your organization's digital resilience, ensuring that it remains strong in the face of evolving threats.

Imagine it as the digital coach that trains your cybersecurity team to be proactive and vigilant in their efforts to detect and classify security incidents.

Consider it as the digital storyteller that helps your organization understand the narrative of a security incident, from its inception to its resolution.

Think of detecting and classifying security incidents as the digital strategist that helps your organization develop proactive measures to prevent future incidents.

Imagine it as the digital medic that tends to the wounds inflicted by a security incident, helping your organization recover and rebuild.

Consider it as the digital advocate that champions the importance of detecting and classifying security incidents as a cornerstone of cybersecurity.

In essence, detecting and classifying security incidents is a vital function that ensures your organization remains vigilant and responsive in the ever-evolving landscape of cyber threats, providing protection and peace of mind in an increasingly digital world.

Next, let's explore the critical process of prioritizing and responding to incidents in the realm of cybersecurity, an essential element in safeguarding your digital assets and maintaining your organization's resilience.

Think of prioritizing and responding to incidents as a well-choreographed dance, where every move is crucial in effectively addressing the myriad of threats that can arise in the digital world.

Consider it as the crisis manager's toolkit, where you have a set of well-defined tools and strategies at your disposal to tackle incidents head-on.

Picture it as a digital chess match, where you need to think several steps ahead to outmaneuver cyber adversaries and protect your organization.

Think of prioritizing and responding to incidents as the conductor's baton, guiding your incident response team in a harmonious effort to minimize the impact of security breaches.

Imagine it as a digital battlefield, where your cybersecurity team is the elite force, ready to engage and counteract threats as they emerge.

Consider it as the navigator's compass, helping your organization find its way through the stormy seas of cybersecurity incidents, ensuring that you reach the shore unscathed.

Think of prioritizing and responding to incidents as the first responder's toolkit, where rapid and well-coordinated actions can mean the difference between containment and catastrophe.

Imagine it as the firefighter's hose, aimed at extinguishing the flames of cyberattacks and preventing them from spreading further.

Consider it as the detective's magnifying glass, helping you uncover the clues and evidence needed to understand the nature and origin of the incident.

Think of prioritizing and responding to incidents as the guardian of your organization's data and reputation, ensuring that you protect what matters most.

Imagine it as the bridge connecting your cybersecurity team with other departments, aligning response efforts with the broader organizational strategy.

Consider it as the crisis communicator's script, guiding your organization in crafting messages that maintain trust and credibility during an incident.

Think of prioritizing and responding to incidents as the triage nurse, assessing the severity of each incident and ensuring that the most critical issues receive immediate attention.

Imagine it as the digital therapist, helping your organization cope with the psychological impact of a security incident and guiding the healing process.

Consider it as the architect's blueprint, outlining the steps and procedures to follow when responding to incidents, ensuring a structured and effective approach.

Think of prioritizing and responding to incidents as the conductor leading an orchestra of security experts, orchestrating their efforts to create a harmonious response.

Imagine it as the crisis negotiator, engaging with threat actors during incidents, seeking to resolve the situation peacefully and with minimal harm.

Consider it as the bridge-builder, fostering collaboration among cybersecurity professionals, incident responders, and other stakeholders, strengthening your collective defense.

Think of prioritizing and responding to incidents as the guardian of your organization's digital resilience, ensuring that you remain strong in the face of adversity.

Imagine it as the coach, training your incident response team to be proactive and effective in their efforts to mitigate the impact of incidents.

Consider it as the storyteller, helping your organization understand the narrative of an incident, from its discovery to its resolution.

Think of prioritizing and responding to incidents as the strategist, developing proactive measures to prevent future incidents and improve your organization's security posture.

Imagine it as the medic, tending to the wounds inflicted by an incident, helping your organization recover and adapt to the evolving threat landscape.

Consider it as the advocate, championing the importance of prioritizing and responding to incidents as a fundamental aspect of cybersecurity.

In essence, prioritizing and responding to incidents is like having a well-orchestrated plan in place, ready to guide your organization through the challenges of the digital world, ensuring that you emerge stronger and more resilient in the face of adversity.

Chapter 6: Advanced Malware Analysis Techniques

Now, let's delve into the intriguing world of code deobfuscation and unpacking, essential skills for anyone involved in malware analysis and cybersecurity.

Think of code deobfuscation and unpacking as the art of unraveling a digital puzzle, where you're deciphering complex and obscured code to reveal its true nature.

Consider it as the cryptographer's challenge, where you're breaking through layers of obfuscation to uncover the hidden secrets within a piece of software.

Picture it as a digital archaeologist's excavation, carefully peeling back the layers of protection to expose the core of a potentially malicious program.

Think of code deobfuscation and unpacking as the detective's magnifying glass, allowing you to examine the inner workings of a binary and understand its functionality.

Imagine it as the locksmith's set of tools, enabling you to unlock the potential of a file that has been intentionally obfuscated to hide its true purpose.

Consider it as the surgeon's scalpel, precision instruments used to dissect and analyze a binary, ensuring that no detail is overlooked.

Think of code deobfuscation and unpacking as the linguist's translation work, converting a foreign and cryptic language into a form that can be understood and analyzed.

Imagine it as the decoder ring for malware, providing insights into the intentions and capabilities of malicious code.

Consider it as the digital detective's toolkit, equipped with techniques to uncover hidden malware features and behaviors.

Think of code deobfuscation and unpacking as the digital locksmith's skillset, able to open the most intricate and well-guarded locks within a binary.

Imagine it as the code surgeon's precision, delicately removing layers of protection while preserving the integrity of the code.

Consider it as the cryptanalyst's challenge, deciphering the cryptographic techniques used to conceal malicious payloads.

Think of code deobfuscation and unpacking as the pathfinder's map, guiding you through the labyrinth of obfuscated code to reach the heart of a binary.

Imagine it as the archaeologist's brush, gently sweeping away the dust of obfuscation to reveal the hidden artifacts of a binary's functionality.

Consider it as the digital explorer's compass, pointing the way to understanding the inner workings of a program.

Think of code deobfuscation and unpacking as the digital detective's toolset, enabling you to piece together the puzzle of a malicious binary.

Imagine it as the locksmith's key, unlocking the potential for deeper analysis and threat assessment.

Consider it as the cryptanalyst's cipher-breaking skills, allowing you to decipher the hidden messages within a piece of obfuscated code.

Think of code deobfuscation and unpacking as the codebreaker's challenge, where you're tasked with unraveling the encryption and obfuscation techniques employed by malware authors.

Imagine it as the digital sleuth's toolkit, equipped with techniques to reveal the true intent and functionality of a piece of malicious code.

Consider it as the archaeologist's excavation tools, carefully uncovering the layers of obfuscation to expose the underlying structure and logic of a binary.

Think of code deobfuscation and unpacking as the digital locksmith's skill, capable of opening the most intricate and well-protected locks within a binary.

Imagine it as the surgeon's scalpel, used with precision to dissect and analyze a binary's code, revealing its hidden secrets.

Consider it as the codebreaker's codebook, filled with techniques and strategies for deciphering the complex and obfuscated code used by malware authors.

In essence, code deobfuscation and unpacking are like the keys to unlocking the mysteries hidden within malware, allowing cybersecurity professionals and malware analysts to understand and combat digital threats more effectively.

Now, let's dive into the fascinating world of malware persistence mechanisms analysis, a crucial aspect of understanding how malicious software maintains its foothold in compromised systems.

Think of malware persistence as the tenacity of an unwelcome guest who refuses to leave your digital premises, continually finding ways to stay, even after you've shown them the door.

Consider it as a game of hide and seek, where the malware plays the role of the elusive hider, and your job is to uncover its hiding spots within the system.

Picture it as a battle of wits between the defender and the attacker, where the malware employs various tricks to maintain access, and you strive to detect and eliminate those persistent hooks.

Think of malware persistence mechanisms analysis as the detective's pursuit of a criminal who always manages to slip away, leaving behind subtle clues that require careful examination.

Imagine it as the exploration of secret passages within a digital fortress, seeking hidden entrances that enable malware to sneak back in.

Consider it as the gardener's diligent inspection for weeds in a well-tended garden, removing any persistent threats to the healthy ecosystem of your system.

Think of malware persistence as a stubborn stain on a white shirt, where conventional cleaning methods may not suffice, and you must employ specialized techniques to remove it completely.

Imagine it as a cat-and-mouse game, with the malware constantly adapting to your defenses, and your response requiring agility and innovation.

Consider it as the archaeologist's excavation of ancient ruins, carefully uncovering the layers of obfuscation to reveal the underlying structure of the malware's persistence.

Think of malware persistence mechanisms analysis as the locksmith's scrutiny of a lock, examining each pin and tumbler to understand how it operates and how to pick it.

Imagine it as a puzzle, with each piece representing a different facet of the malware's persistence, and your task is to assemble them to see the bigger picture.

Consider it as a chess match, where the malware makes strategic moves to maintain its presence, and your response requires thoughtful and strategic counterplays.

Think of malware persistence as a relentless adversary, always looking for new ways to infiltrate and persist, and your role is to stay one step ahead in the ongoing battle.

Imagine it as the explorer's quest for hidden treasures within a vast jungle, where the treasures are the clues to understanding how malware maintains its hold.

Consider it as the gardener's vigilance in protecting a garden from persistent pests, implementing measures to prevent their return.

Think of malware persistence mechanisms analysis as a continuous process, where new techniques emerge as malware authors adapt to security measures, and you must remain vigilant and proactive.

Imagine it as a journey of discovery, where each new finding about a malware's persistence mechanism adds to your knowledge and strengthens your ability to defend against future threats.

Consider it as a cat-and-mouse chase in a digital maze, with the malware trying to elude your grasp, and your determination to corner it and remove its persistence.

Think of malware persistence as a shadowy figure lurking in the background, and your analysis as shining a light on its activities, exposing its presence.

Imagine it as a puzzle with missing pieces, where your analysis gradually fills in the gaps and reveals the complete picture of how malware maintains its persistence.

Consider it as the gardener's commitment to maintaining a healthy and pest-free environment, ensuring that persistent threats are identified and eliminated.

In essence, malware persistence mechanisms analysis is like being a vigilant guardian of your digital domain, constantly seeking out and removing the hidden hooks that malware uses to maintain access, ensuring the security and integrity of your systems.

Chapter 7: Memory Forensics and Volatile Data Analysis

Of course, let's delve into the intriguing realm of analyzing RAM (Random Access Memory) artifacts for malware, a fascinating aspect of digital forensics and malware analysis that allows us to uncover valuable insights into a system's current state and potential security breaches.

Think of RAM as the digital brain of a computer, where active processes, data, and even pieces of malware are temporarily stored while the system is running.

Consider RAM artifacts as the footprints left behind by these processes and malware, akin to clues at a crime scene that can help us reconstruct events and identify malicious activities.

Picture it as a digital treasure hunt, where we explore the volatile memory of a computer to discover hidden gems of information that may hold the key to understanding and mitigating malware threats.

Think of analyzing RAM artifacts as a journey into the inner workings of a system, providing us with a real-time snapshot of what is happening within, including any unwelcome guests like malware.

Imagine it as an archaeological expedition, where we carefully unearth and examine the layers of memory to reveal the historical record of a system's activities, including malware interactions.

Consider RAM analysis as the digital equivalent of examining fingerprints, where each artifact can uniquely identify a process or malware and help us piece together the puzzle of an incident.

Think of RAM artifacts as the breadcrumbs left behind in a digital forest, guiding us through the events and processes that have occurred on a system, including malware executions.

Imagine it as a detective's toolkit, complete with magnifying glass and forensic tools, allowing us to scrutinize the volatile memory for any traces of malicious intent.

Consider RAM analysis as a continuous monitoring process, where we keep a vigilant eye on a system's memory to quickly detect and respond to any malware activity.

Think of it as an ongoing dialogue with a system, listening for whispers of malicious code and understanding its behavior through the artifacts it leaves behind in RAM.

Imagine RAM analysis as a backstage pass to the inner workings of a computer, granting us access to the real-time actions of processes and, potentially, the stealthy movements of malware.

Consider it as the detective's interview with a witness, where the RAM artifacts provide valuable testimony about what happened during a security incident.

Think of RAM analysis as a dynamic process, evolving with the system's state, and allowing us to adapt our strategies to uncover new insights into malware behavior.

Imagine it as a digital MRI scan, revealing the hidden structures and processes within a computer's memory, including any malicious anomalies.

Consider RAM analysis as a guardian's watchful eye, ensuring that the system remains free from the influence of malware by promptly detecting and responding to any threats.

Think of it as a virtual microscope, magnifying the details within RAM to reveal the intricacies of malware behavior and execution.

Imagine RAM artifacts as the breadcrumbs that can lead us to the heart of a security incident, helping us understand how malware entered, operated, and potentially exfiltrated data from a system.

Consider it as the digital archaeologist's meticulous excavation, sifting through layers of memory to unearth the hidden artifacts of malware presence and activity.

Think of RAM analysis as a continuous learning process, where each encounter with malware artifacts enhances our understanding and ability to protect against future threats.

Imagine it as a journey into the digital wilderness, where we follow the tracks of malware through RAM to discover its origins, motives, and potential impact.

Consider RAM analysis as a dynamic conversation with the system's memory, deciphering the messages left behind by processes and malware to better safeguard against future intrusions.

In essence, analyzing RAM artifacts for malware is akin to being a vigilant sentinel, guarding the digital realm by uncovering the hidden traces of malicious activity and ensuring the security and integrity of computer systems.

Next, let's delve into the fascinating world of identifying memory-resident malicious processes, a critical aspect of malware analysis and cybersecurity that plays a pivotal role in safeguarding digital environments from threats.

Picture memory-resident malicious processes as stealthy infiltrators lurking within the heart of a computer's RAM, where they hide, operate, and potentially wreak havoc.

Think of them as digital spies, camouflaged among legitimate processes, quietly collecting data, executing commands, and evading detection by security measures.

Consider identifying these memory-resident threats as a high-stakes game of hide and seek, where the stakes are the security and integrity of the system, and the adversaries are cleverly concealed within the volatile memory.

Imagine it as a detective's challenge, where we must sift through the dynamic landscape of RAM to pinpoint the telltale signs of malicious activity.

Think of memory-resident malware as digital chameleons, adapting to their surroundings and often leaving only subtle traces that require expert analysis to uncover.

Consider the process of identification as akin to decoding a puzzle, where each piece of evidence, such as unusual behavior or unexpected system changes, helps us put together the bigger picture of a potential threat.

Imagine it as a digital battlefield, where we engage in a constant cat-and-mouse game with malicious processes, working tirelessly to detect and neutralize them.

Think of identifying memory-resident malware as peeling back the layers of an onion, revealing the concealed, inner workings of these threats as we progressively analyze their activities.

Consider it as the digital equivalent of medical diagnosis, where we observe symptoms and patterns in memory to identify the underlying ailment, which, in this case, is the presence of malicious processes.

Imagine it as a dynamic dialogue between the system and the analyst, where we carefully listen to the cues provided by the system's memory, looking for any hints of abnormal behavior that may indicate malware.

Think of identifying memory-resident threats as a digital treasure hunt, where each clue, no matter how subtle, leads us closer to uncovering the hidden malware.

Consider it as a continuous surveillance operation, where we maintain constant vigilance over the system's memory, watching for any anomalies that could signal the presence of malicious processes.

Imagine it as a digital fingerprint analysis, where we compare the behavioral patterns of known malware with the activities observed in RAM to make an accurate identification.

Think of the identification process as a complex puzzle, where we must piece together information from various sources, including system logs, memory dumps, and behavioral analysis, to reveal the full picture.

Consider it as a digital forensics expedition, where we explore the volatile memory landscape for clues that can lead us to the memory-resident malware's lair.

Imagine it as a conversation between the analyst and the system, with the memory acting as the witness, providing critical information about any suspicious processes it has encountered.

Think of identifying memory-resident malicious processes as a detective's art, requiring a keen eye for detail, a deep understanding of system behavior, and a commitment to staying one step ahead of cyber adversaries.

Consider it as a dynamic dance between security measures and malware, where we continually adapt our techniques to outmaneuver and expose the hidden threats.

Imagine it as a digital game of chess, where we strategically analyze the memory to anticipate the moves of memory-resident malware and counter their actions effectively.

Think of the identification process as a crucial step in the larger cybersecurity strategy, where early detection can prevent potential breaches and minimize the impact of malicious processes.

Consider it as a digital guardian's duty, protecting the integrity and security of digital environments by tirelessly searching for and neutralizing memory-resident threats.

Imagine it as a journey into the digital unknown, where each identification of memory-resident malware brings us closer to a safer and more secure digital world.

In essence, identifying memory-resident malicious processes is both an art and a science, a vital skill in the ever-evolving landscape of cybersecurity, where diligence, expertise, and constant vigilance are our greatest allies against the hidden threats lurking within the volatile memory of our digital systems.

Chapter 8: Network Forensics and Traffic Analysis

Now, let's explore the intriguing realm of packet capture and analysis, a fundamental aspect of network security and digital forensics that offers valuable insights into the flow of data within computer networks. Think of packet capture as a digital telescope, allowing us to peer into the intricate world of network communication, where data travels in discrete, bite-sized units known as packets.

Consider it as the equivalent of intercepting and decoding messages in a secret language, where each packet holds a piece of the conversation between devices on the network.

Imagine it as eavesdropping on the digital conversations happening all around us, with each packet revealing its origins, destination, content, and purpose.

Think of packet capture as a window into the digital realm, where we can observe the exchange of information, commands, and data between computers, servers, and devices.

Consider it as a digital detective's tool, enabling us to uncover the hidden narratives within the vast sea of network traffic.

Imagine it as the equivalent of taking snapshots of traffic on a busy highway, with each packet representing a vehicle carrying data from one point to another.

Think of packet capture as a digital net, capturing the data fish swimming through the vast ocean of network communication, allowing us to examine them closely.

Consider it as a backstage pass to the inner workings of the digital world, where we can see how data flows, who it's coming from, and where it's going.

Imagine it as a journey through the digital wilderness, where each packet is a footprint, guiding us to a better understanding of the network's behavior.

Think of packet analysis as decoding a digital puzzle, where we piece together the packets to reconstruct the full picture of a network conversation.

Consider it as a linguistic analysis of the digital language, where we decipher the meaning behind the packets' headers and payloads.

Imagine it as a treasure hunt, where we follow the trail of packets to uncover hidden gems of information, such as passwords, commands, or vulnerabilities.

Think of packet capture and analysis as a digital microscope, allowing us to zoom in on the tiniest details of network traffic to detect anomalies or threats.

Consider it as a journey through time, as we replay captured packets to see the sequence of events leading up to a network incident.

Imagine it as a digital conversation between devices, where packets are the words and phrases exchanged to accomplish various tasks.

Think of packet analysis as digital forensics, where we investigate network activity to understand what happened, why, and who was involved.

Consider it as a tool for troubleshooting network issues, as we examine packets to identify bottlenecks, errors, or misconfigurations.

Imagine it as a digital mirror reflecting the health and security of a network, revealing its strengths and weaknesses. Think of packet capture as a witness to digital events, providing an unbiased account of network activities that can be used in legal cases or incident response. Consider it as a tool for improving network performance, as we analyze packets to optimize data transfer and reduce latency.

Imagine it as a digital conversation between devices, where packets convey not only data but also intentions, intentions that can be benign or malicious.

Think of packet capture as a valuable resource for threat detection, allowing us to spot patterns of suspicious behavior or intrusion attempts.

Consider it as a digital guardian, protecting the network by identifying and neutralizing potential threats.

Imagine it as a digital storyteller, narrating the tale of network traffic, with each packet adding a new chapter to the narrative. Think of packet analysis as a means of ensuring compliance with security policies and regulations, as we monitor packets for unauthorized activities or data breaches.

Consider it as a way to enhance network security by identifying and blocking malicious packets in real-time.

Imagine it as a digital librarian, organizing and categorizing packets to make sense of the vast amount of network data.

Think of packet capture and analysis as a fundamental skill in the field of cybersecurity and digital forensics, where expertise in deciphering the language of packets is essential for safeguarding networks and investigating incidents.

Consider it as a never-ending journey of discovery, where each packet tells a story, and every analysis deepens our understanding of the digital world.

Imagine it as a partnership between humans and technology, where our curiosity and expertise combine with powerful tools to keep the digital realm secure and reliable.

In essence, packet capture and analysis are not just technical processes but a gateway to the hidden world of network communication, where every packet carries a piece of the digital conversation, waiting to be decoded and understood by those dedicated to the art and science of cybersecurity and digital forensics.

Let's delve into the fascinating world of detecting malicious patterns in network traffic, a crucial aspect of cybersecurity that involves identifying and mitigating threats lurking within the vast data flows of computer networks.

Imagine network traffic as a bustling city, where data packets zip around like vehicles on a complex highway system, each with its own purpose and destination.

Think of detecting malicious patterns as the work of vigilant traffic police, meticulously observing the flow of packets to spot any suspicious or unlawful activity.

Consider network traffic as a digital ecosystem, where legitimate data exchanges coexist with potential threats, forming a rich tapestry of information.

Picture the task of detection as akin to finding needles in a haystack, with malicious patterns hiding amidst the legitimate ones, waiting to be uncovered.

Imagine it as a game of cat and mouse, where cybercriminals constantly evolve their tactics, and security professionals strive to stay one step ahead.

Consider detecting malicious patterns as a digital detective's mission, where every clue is a packet, and every anomaly is a potential lead.

Think of network traffic analysis as a puzzle, where the pieces are packets, and the picture is a complete understanding of what's happening within the network.

Consider it as a journey through a digital labyrinth, with each packet containing clues about the intentions and actions of devices on the network.

Imagine it as a symphony of data, where packets play different roles in a complex composition, and detecting malicious patterns is like recognizing a discordant note in the harmony.

Think of network traffic as a language, with packets serving as words, and detecting malicious patterns is like deciphering a hidden message within the conversation.

Consider it as a safeguard for the digital world, where the detection of malicious patterns can prevent data breaches, cyberattacks, and other security incidents.

Imagine it as a radar system, scanning the digital airspace for any signs of intruders or anomalies.

Think of detecting malicious patterns as a filter, separating legitimate network activities from potentially harmful ones.

Consider it as a virtual watchtower, where security professionals keep a vigilant eye on the network's traffic to protect it from threats.

Imagine it as a cat-and-mouse game, where cybercriminals constantly adapt and security experts work tirelessly to uncover their tactics.

Think of detecting malicious patterns as a digital guardian, defending the network against unseen threats and vulnerabilities.

Consider it as a journey through the digital wilderness, where every packet holds a clue that can lead to the discovery of malicious activity.

Imagine it as a digital microscope, allowing us to zoom in on the smallest details of network traffic to identify irregularities.

Think of network traffic as a river of data, and detecting malicious patterns as fishing for threats within its currents.

Consider it as a puzzle-solving endeavor, where each piece of data contributes to a clearer picture of the network's security.

Imagine it as a conversation between devices, where packets are the words, and detecting malicious patterns is like understanding the hidden meaning in their dialogue.

Think of it as a digital forensics investigation, where every packet is a piece of evidence that can reveal the nature and source of a security threat.

Consider it as a form of digital hygiene, where regular scanning for malicious patterns helps keep the network healthy and secure.

Imagine it as a digital guardian angel, watching over the network to ensure its safety and integrity.

Think of detecting malicious patterns as a continuous process, where security professionals must adapt and evolve to stay ahead of ever-changing threats.

Consider it as a digital cat burglar alarm, ready to sound at the slightest hint of suspicious activity.

Imagine it as a digital detective agency, where analysts sift through vast amounts of data to uncover the truth behind network anomalies.

Think of it as a digital battlefield, where security professionals defend against cyberattacks by detecting and mitigating malicious patterns.

Consider detecting malicious patterns as a vital skill in the ever-evolving field of cybersecurity, where constant vigilance and adaptability are paramount.

Imagine it as a partnership between humans and technology, where advanced tools and human expertise work together to keep the digital realm safe from harm.

In essence, detecting malicious patterns in network traffic is a critical task in the ongoing battle to protect our digital world. It requires constant vigilance, adaptability, and a deep understanding of the evolving tactics of cybercriminals. It is the work of digital guardians, safeguarding the integrity and security of our networks in an increasingly complex and interconnected digital landscape.

Chapter 9: Advanced Threat Hunting

Of course, let's dive into the fascinating world of proactive threat hunting methodologies—a proactive approach to cybersecurity that's akin to a digital treasure hunt with a vital mission at its core.

Imagine you're an intrepid explorer, venturing into the vast and sometimes treacherous landscape of your organization's network.

Think of proactive threat hunting as your trusty map and compass, guiding you through the digital wilderness to uncover hidden dangers before they can strike.

Consider it as a digital Sherlock Holmes investigation, where you're constantly on the lookout for clues that could reveal the presence of lurking adversaries.

Imagine it as a game of chess, where you're anticipating the moves of potential threats and strategizing your counter-moves.

Think of proactive threat hunting as a proactive rather than reactive approach, focused on staying one step ahead of cybercriminals.

Consider it as a proactive security posture, where you're actively seeking out vulnerabilities and weaknesses in your network's defenses.

Imagine it as a journey of discovery, where you're peeling back the layers of your network to reveal potential threats hiding beneath the surface.

Think of proactive threat hunting as a continuous process, where you're always on the lookout for signs of compromise.

Consider it as a digital detective's work, where you're piecing together evidence to uncover the full story of a potential threat.

Imagine it as a digital scavenger hunt, where you're searching for hidden treasures (in this case, vulnerabilities and threats).

Think of proactive threat hunting as a proactive stance against cyber threats, rather than waiting for alerts or incidents to occur.

Consider it as a digital guardian, watching over your organization's assets and data with unwavering vigilance.

Imagine it as a proactive reconnaissance mission, where you're gathering intelligence on potential threats in your network.

Think of proactive threat hunting as a crucial part of a robust cybersecurity strategy, complementing your defense-in-depth approach.

Consider it as a proactive and dynamic approach, adapting to the evolving tactics and techniques of cyber adversaries.

Imagine it as a digital safari, where you're tracking and observing elusive cyber threats in their natural habitat.

Think of proactive threat hunting as a proactive measure to reduce the dwell time of threats in your network.

Consider it as a digital forensics investigation, where you're piecing together the timeline of a potential breach.

Imagine it as a proactive security exercise, testing the resilience of your network against a variety of potential threats.

Think of proactive threat hunting as a proactive mindset, instilling a culture of security awareness throughout your organization.

Consider it as a proactive risk mitigation strategy, identifying and addressing vulnerabilities before they can be exploited.

Imagine it as a digital early warning system, alerting you to potential threats before they can cause significant damage.

Think of proactive threat hunting as a proactive stance against cyber threats, minimizing the impact of incidents when they do occur.

Consider it as a digital neighborhood watch program, where you and your security team are vigilant protectors of your network.

Imagine it as a proactive strategy to protect your organization's reputation and customer trust.

Think of proactive threat hunting as a continuous improvement process, refining your techniques and strategies over time.

Consider it as a proactive effort to stay ahead of emerging threats in the ever-evolving landscape of cybersecurity.

Imagine it as a digital guardian angel, watching over your organization's digital assets and data with unwavering dedication.

Think of proactive threat hunting as a proactive approach that empowers you to take control of your network's security.

Consider it as a proactive and strategic investment in the long-term resilience of your organization.

Imagine it as a digital partnership between humans and technology, with advanced tools and human expertise working hand in hand.

Think of proactive threat hunting as a proactive measure that helps you sleep better at night, knowing that you're actively safeguarding your organization from potential threats.

Consider it as a proactive and forward-thinking approach that sets your organization on the path to a more secure and resilient future.

In essence, proactive threat hunting methodologies are a proactive and strategic approach to cybersecurity, allowing organizations to actively seek out and mitigate potential threats before they can cause harm. It's a proactive stance against cyber adversaries, a continuous improvement process, and a vital component of a robust cybersecurity strategy. With the right tools, expertise, and mindset, proactive threat hunting empowers organizations to take control of their security and protect their digital assets from evolving threats in the ever-changing landscape of cybersecurity.

Next, let's delve into the crucial topic of analyzing Indicators of Compromise (IOCs) and how they play a pivotal role in modern cybersecurity.

Imagine IOCs as breadcrumbs left behind by a digital intruder, tiny clues that can lead you to the heart of a cybercrime mystery.

Think of IOCs as digital fingerprints, unique identifiers that can help you track and trace the actions of a cyber adversary.

Consider them as the telltale signs of a security incident, valuable pieces of evidence that can help you uncover the scope and impact of an attack.

Imagine IOCs as the keys to unlocking the secrets of a cyber intrusion, providing insights into the tactics, techniques, and procedures (TTPs) of malicious actors.

Think of them as the early warning signs of a potential breach, allowing you to take swift action to protect your organization's assets.

Consider IOCs as the building blocks of threat intelligence, essential elements that help you understand the ever-evolving threat landscape.

Imagine them as digital footprints, left by cybercriminals as they navigate your network, leaving behind traces of their activities.

Think of IOCs as a digital detective's toolkit, filled with clues that can help you piece together the puzzle of a cyber attack.

Consider them as the signposts of the digital world, guiding you toward potential threats and vulnerabilities.

Imagine IOCs as the breadcrumbs that lead you out of the dark forest of cyber threats and toward the safety of a secure network.

Think of them as the alarm bells that ring when something suspicious is happening in your digital domain.

Consider IOCs as the markers on a treasure map, guiding you to hidden dangers and valuable insights.

Imagine them as the early warning system of the digital realm, alerting you to potential threats before they can cause harm.

Think of IOCs as the puzzle pieces that, when assembled, reveal the big picture of a security incident.

Consider them as the thread that unravels the web of cyber deception, exposing the true nature of an attack.

Imagine IOCs as the clues that lead you to the heart of a cybercrime mystery, allowing you to understand how, when, and where the attack occurred.

Think of them as the digital breadcrumbs that lead you to the source of a security breach, helping you plug the leak and secure your systems.

Consider IOCs as the keys to the digital kingdom, granting you access to the insights and knowledge needed to defend against cyber threats.

Imagine them as the digital signatures of malicious activity, allowing you to spot anomalies and anomalies in your network.

Think of IOCs as the smoke signals of the digital age, alerting you to potential fires before they rage out of control.

Consider them as the markers on a digital map, guiding you toward the safe harbor of a secure network.

Imagine IOCs as the early warning system that helps you stay one step ahead of cyber adversaries, anticipating their moves and thwarting their plans.

Think of them as the breadcrumbs that lead you to the heart of a cybercrime investigation, allowing you to gather evidence and build a case.

Consider IOCs as the digital clues that reveal the modus operandi of a cyber adversary, shedding light on their tactics and techniques.

Imagine them as the warning signs on the road of digital security, helping you navigate the twists and turns of the cyber threat landscape.

Think of IOCs as the digital tracks left by a cybercriminal, allowing you to follow their trail and apprehend them.

Consider them as the digital footprints that lead you to the hidden lairs of cyber adversaries, exposing their infrastructure and operations.

Imagine IOCs as the keys to the kingdom of threat intelligence, empowering you to make informed decisions and take proactive measures to protect your organization.

Think of them as the breadcrumbs that lead you to the heart of a cybersecurity investigation, where you unravel the mysteries of the digital world.

Consider IOCs as the digital breadcrumbs that, when followed, lead you to the truth of a security incident, helping you respond effectively and mitigate the impact.

In essence, analyzing Indicators of Compromise (IOCs) is a critical component of modern cybersecurity. These digital breadcrumbs, left behind by cyber adversaries, are essential for identifying and understanding security incidents, allowing organizations to take swift and informed action to protect their assets. IOCs are the keys to unraveling the mysteries of cyber attacks, guiding cybersecurity professionals toward the heart of the threat and helping them respond effectively to mitigate the impact. They are the digital clues, the warning signs, and the early warning system that empowers organizations to stay one step ahead of cyber adversaries in the ever-evolving landscape of cybersecurity.

Chapter 10: Post-Incident Analysis and Remediation

Next, let's explore the crucial process of conducting a root cause analysis of security incidents in the world of cybersecurity.

Root cause analysis is like peeling back the layers of an onion, going beyond the surface to uncover the underlying factors that led to a security incident.

It's akin to being a digital detective, searching for clues and evidence to understand how and why a security breach occurred.

Imagine it as a journey into the heart of a cybersecurity incident, where you aim to discover the core issues that allowed the breach to happen.

Think of root cause analysis as a proactive approach to cybersecurity, helping organizations not only respond to incidents but also prevent them from happening again.

It's like solving a puzzle, where each piece of information you gather brings you closer to understanding the complete picture.

Root cause analysis is all about asking the right questions, delving deep into the incident's timeline, and examining all relevant data.

Imagine it as a voyage of discovery, where you navigate through logs, forensic evidence, and incident reports to find the root causes.

Think of it as a journey into the digital realm, where you seek to uncover the hidden vulnerabilities and weaknesses in your cybersecurity defenses.

Root cause analysis is not about placing blame but about finding solutions and making improvements to prevent future incidents.

It's like a medical diagnosis, where you identify the underlying illness to prescribe the right treatment.

Imagine it as a form of introspection for your organization, where you reflect on what went wrong and how to make things right.

Think of it as a continuous improvement process, where each incident becomes an opportunity to strengthen your cybersecurity posture.

Root cause analysis involves a systematic approach, starting with the identification of the incident's symptoms and working backward to find the root causes.

It's like solving a mystery, where you gather evidence, interview witnesses, and reconstruct the sequence of events.

Imagine it as a journey into the past, where you rewind the digital clock to understand the chain of events leading up to the incident.

Think of it as a quest for knowledge, where you seek to understand not only what happened but why it happened.

Root cause analysis requires collaboration among various teams, from IT and security to management and legal.

It's like assembling a team of experts, each contributing their knowledge and skills to unravel the incident's complexities.

Imagine it as a collective effort, where everyone works together to find the answers and implement preventive measures.

Think of it as a learning experience, where each incident teaches valuable lessons that can be applied to future cybersecurity strategies.

Root cause analysis involves documenting the findings, creating incident reports, and implementing corrective actions.

It's like building a roadmap for improvement, where you outline the steps needed to prevent similar incidents in the future.

Imagine it as a blueprint for resilience, where you fortify your defenses based on the vulnerabilities exposed during the analysis.

Think of it as an investment in your organization's cybersecurity maturity, where each incident becomes an opportunity for growth.

Root cause analysis is not a one-time process but a continuous cycle of improvement, where lessons learned from one incident inform future strategies.

It's like a feedback loop, where the insights gained from each analysis feed into the development of stronger cybersecurity defenses.

Imagine it as a journey of evolution, where your organization becomes more resilient and adaptive in the face of emerging threats.

Think of it as a commitment to excellence in cybersecurity, where you strive to stay ahead of cyber adversaries by addressing root causes.

Root cause analysis is not only about addressing the symptoms of security incidents but also about addressing the underlying issues that can lead to future breaches.

It's like tending to the root of a tree, ensuring its health and stability to withstand future storms.

Imagine it as a proactive approach to cybersecurity, where you take control of your organization's digital destiny.

Think of it as a strategic investment in your organization's future, where each incident analysis contributes to a stronger and more secure cybersecurity posture.

In summary, root cause analysis of security incidents is an essential practice in modern cybersecurity. It's a process of deep exploration, investigation, and learning that goes beyond the surface to uncover the underlying factors that lead to incidents. Root cause analysis is not about blame but about finding solutions and making improvements to prevent future incidents. It's a proactive and collaborative effort that involves multiple teams and results in actionable insights and enhanced cybersecurity resilience. It's a continuous cycle of improvement that helps organizations stay ahead of emerging threats and build a stronger, more secure digital future.

of cybersecurity.

Remediation is like the healing process after an injury, where the goal is to recover, strengthen, and prevent future harm to the body.

It's akin to restoring a damaged fortress, reinforcing its defenses to withstand future attacks.

Imagine it as a rehabilitation program for your digital environment, aimed at recovering from security incidents and fortifying your defenses.

Think of remediation as the art of turning vulnerabilities into strengths, using each incident as an opportunity to improve your cybersecurity posture.

Remediation is not just about fixing what's broken; it's about building a more resilient and adaptive cybersecurity ecosystem.

It's like renovating a house, where you not only repair the damage but also enhance its overall security and functionality.

Imagine it as an ongoing commitment to cybersecurity excellence, where you continually strengthen your defenses against evolving threats.

Think of remediation as a journey of improvement, where each step forward brings you closer to a more secure digital future.

Effective remediation starts with a thorough assessment of the incident's impact and scope.

It's like a medical examination, where you diagnose the extent of the injury before prescribing a treatment plan.

Imagine it as a fact-finding mission, where you gather data and evidence to understand the incident's implications fully.

Think of it as a critical first step, where you gain clarity on what needs to be addressed and how to proceed.

Remediation involves prioritizing actions based on the severity of the vulnerabilities discovered.

It's like triage in a medical emergency, where you focus on treating the most critical issues first.

Imagine it as a strategic approach, where you allocate resources wisely to mitigate the most significant risks promptly.

Think of it as a calculated response, where you address the most pressing concerns to prevent further damage.

Effective remediation requires a multidisciplinary team, including IT, security, legal, and management.

It's like a well-coordinated orchestra, where each instrument plays a crucial role in achieving harmony.

Imagine it as a collaborative effort, where everyone brings their expertise to the table to resolve the incident comprehensively.

Think of it as a collective commitment, where the entire organization works together towards a common goal.

Remediation is not just about patching vulnerabilities; it's about addressing the root causes.

It's like treating the source of an illness rather than just the symptoms.

Imagine it as a detective's work, where you uncover the underlying issues that led to the incident.

Think of it as a process of discovery, where you strive to prevent similar incidents in the future.

Remediation strategies include applying security patches, updating software, and enhancing access controls.

It's like upgrading your home security system, installing stronger locks and alarms to deter burglars.

Imagine it as strengthening your digital fortress, making it harder for cyber adversaries to breach your defenses.

Think of it as a proactive approach, where you eliminate vulnerabilities before they can be exploited.

Effective remediation also involves continuous monitoring and testing to ensure the effectiveness of security measures.

It's like conducting fire drills to ensure everyone knows what to do in case of an emergency.

Imagine it as a practice of readiness, where you stay vigilant and prepared for potential threats.

Think of it as a commitment to ongoing improvement, where you refine your security posture based on real-world experiences.

Remediation extends beyond technical measures; it also includes educating and raising awareness among employees.

It's like teaching people to recognize and respond to potential dangers in their environment.

Imagine it as a culture of security, where every member of the organization plays a role in safeguarding its digital assets.

Think of it as a shared responsibility, where cybersecurity becomes a collective effort.

Remediation is not a one-time process but a continuous cycle of improvement.

It's like maintaining a garden, where you tend to it regularly to ensure its health and vitality.

Imagine it as a commitment to long-term resilience, where you adapt and evolve to stay ahead of emerging threats.

Think of it as a journey of growth, where each remediation effort contributes to a more secure digital landscape.

In summary, remediation strategies and best practices are essential components of effective cybersecurity. Remediation is not just about fixing vulnerabilities; it's about strengthening and fortifying your digital defenses. It involves a thorough assessment, prioritization of actions, collaboration among teams, and a commitment to ongoing improvement. Remediation addresses not only technical issues but also cultural and educational aspects of cybersecurity. It's a continuous cycle of enhancement that helps organizations adapt and evolve in the ever-changing threat landscape. Ultimately, remediation is about turning vulnerabilities into strengths and building a more secure digital future.

BOOK 4
EXPERT MALWARE ANALYSIS AND DIGITAL FORENSICS
MASTERING CYBERSECURITY INCIDENT RESPONSE

ROB BOTWRIGHT

Chapter 1: Cyber Threats in the Modern Landscape

Next, let's explore the ever-evolving landscape of emerging cyber threat trends.

In today's interconnected world, where technology plays an integral role in our daily lives, the threat landscape is constantly evolving, presenting new challenges and opportunities for cybercriminals and cybersecurity professionals alike.

One of the most prominent emerging threats is the rise of ransomware attacks, where cybercriminals encrypt an organization's data and demand a ransom for its release.

These attacks have become more sophisticated, with threat actors targeting critical infrastructure, healthcare organizations, and even municipalities, causing significant disruptions and financial losses.

Ransomware-as-a-Service (RaaS) platforms have also emerged, making it easier for less technically skilled criminals to carry out attacks, further increasing the threat.

Another concerning trend is the growing prevalence of supply chain attacks, where cybercriminals target software vendors or service providers to infiltrate their customers' networks.

This tactic allows threat actors to compromise multiple organizations through a single point of entry, making these attacks particularly dangerous.

SolarWinds, a prominent example, suffered a breach that affected thousands of its customers, demonstrating the far-reaching impact of supply chain attacks.

The Internet of Things (IoT) continues to be a fertile ground for cyber threats, with the proliferation of connected devices in homes and businesses.

Weak security measures in many IoT devices make them susceptible to exploitation, leading to botnets, distributed denial-of-service (DDoS) attacks, and data breaches.

As more critical infrastructure relies on IoT technology, the potential consequences of these attacks become increasingly severe.

Cyber espionage by nation-state actors remains a significant concern, with countries engaging in covert operations to steal intellectual property, sensitive government information, and conduct influence campaigns.

Attribution in these cases is challenging, as advanced persistent threat (APT) groups employ sophisticated techniques to mask their origins.

In recent years, the lines between cybercriminals and nation-state actors have blurred, as some APT groups engage in financially motivated attacks alongside traditional espionage activities.

The proliferation of cryptocurrency has facilitated cybercrime, as it provides an anonymous and decentralized means of conducting financial transactions.

Ransomware payments are often demanded in cryptocurrency, making it difficult for law enforcement to trace and apprehend cybercriminals.

Additionally, cybercriminals have increasingly turned to cryptocurrency mining malware to monetize their activities, using victims' computing resources to mine cryptocurrency without their knowledge or consent.

Cloud services have become integral to modern business operations, but they also present new attack surfaces for cybercriminals.

Misconfigured cloud storage and weak access controls have led to data breaches and exposure of sensitive information.

Organizations must carefully manage their cloud security to mitigate these risks.

The adoption of artificial intelligence (AI) and machine learning (ML) in cybersecurity has given rise to a new breed of threats.

Adversarial machine learning techniques enable attackers to manipulate AI algorithms, causing false positives or negatives in security systems.

Moreover, AI-powered attacks can automate and scale cyber threats, making them more effective and challenging to detect.

Social engineering attacks, such as phishing, continue to evolve, with cybercriminals using increasingly convincing tactics to deceive individuals and gain unauthorized access to sensitive information.

Phishing attacks often leverage current events, emotions, and personalization to trick victims into clicking on malicious links or providing confidential data.

Deepfake technology, which uses AI to create realistic but fabricated audio and video content, poses a growing threat in the realm of misinformation and social engineering.

The rise of remote work and the use of personal devices for business purposes have expanded the attack surface for cybercriminals.

Home networks and personal devices may lack the robust security measures of corporate environments, making them vulnerable to exploitation.

Employees also face increased phishing attempts and other social engineering attacks as cybercriminals seek to capitalize on remote work vulnerabilities.

As organizations continue to transition to hybrid and remote work models, securing this distributed workforce remains a top priority.

Cybersecurity professionals must adapt to these emerging threat trends by staying informed about the evolving threat landscape, investing in advanced security solutions, and continuously improving security awareness and training programs.

Collaboration among organizations, information sharing, and threat intelligence sharing also play critical roles in defending against emerging threats.

Ultimately, the fight against cyber threats is an ongoing battle, and staying vigilant and proactive is essential in safeguarding digital assets and maintaining a resilient cybersecurity posture.

Next, let's delve into the profound impact of nation-state threat actors in the realm of cybersecurity.

In the ever-evolving landscape of cybersecurity, nation-state threat actors hold a unique and often daunting position. These sophisticated and well-funded entities, operating with the backing of governments, pose significant challenges to the security of nations, organizations, and individuals alike.

Nation-state threat actors, also known as Advanced Persistent Threat (APT) groups, are typically state-sponsored or state-affiliated organizations or individuals with advanced technical capabilities and extensive resources at their disposal. Their primary objectives can vary widely, encompassing intelligence gathering, espionage, political influence, economic disruption, and even cyber warfare.

One of the most notable aspects of nation-state threat actors is their ability to conduct long-term, covert operations. Unlike many cybercriminals who seek immediate financial gain, APT groups often pursue strategic goals that may take years to achieve.

These threat actors are highly skilled in exploiting vulnerabilities, conducting reconnaissance, and remaining undetected within their targets' networks. They invest considerable time and effort in crafting sophisticated attack campaigns that can circumvent even the most robust cybersecurity defenses.

One of the most notorious examples of nation-state cyber espionage is the case of Stuxnet. In the late 2000s, it was revealed that the Stuxnet worm was developed by a joint effort between the United States and Israel to disrupt Iran's nuclear program. This malware was designed to target specific industrial control systems and demonstrated the capability of nation-states to create highly specialized and destructive cyber weapons.

The impact of nation-state threat actors can extend far beyond the digital realm. In instances of cyber espionage, stolen intellectual property and sensitive government data can result in significant economic losses and jeopardize national security. The theft of cutting-edge technologies, trade secrets, and military strategies can have severe consequences.

Furthermore, nation-state actors have been known to use cyberattacks to influence political events and sow discord. By infiltrating critical infrastructure, manipulating information, or conducting disinformation campaigns, these actors can disrupt the democratic processes of other nations, creating instability and uncertainty.

The rise of APT groups has prompted governments and organizations worldwide to bolster their cybersecurity efforts. In response, cybersecurity professionals have developed increasingly sophisticated threat detection and mitigation strategies.

Attributing cyberattacks to specific nation-state actors is a challenging endeavor. APT groups often go to great lengths to cover their tracks, using false flags and routing their activities through multiple countries to obfuscate their origins. However, advances in threat intelligence and the collaboration of cybersecurity experts from around the globe have improved the ability to attribute cyberattacks more accurately.

Nation-state threat actors also benefit from the anonymity and reach of the internet. They can operate from anywhere in the world, making it difficult for law enforcement agencies to apprehend or prosecute them. This impunity has emboldened APT groups to continue their operations with relative impunity.

The impact of nation-state threat actors underscores the need for international cooperation and norms in cyberspace. As cyber conflict becomes an increasingly prominent feature of geopolitics, diplomatic efforts to establish rules of engagement and deterrence strategies are critical.

In recent years, there have been calls for international agreements on cybersecurity, akin to arms control treaties in the physical world. These agreements would seek to limit the development and use of cyber weapons by nation-states and promote responsible behavior in cyberspace.

Ultimately, the impact of nation-state threat actors in cybersecurity is profound and multifaceted. Their capabilities, objectives, and tactics continue to evolve, posing complex challenges that require ongoing vigilance and collaboration among governments, organizations, and cybersecurity professionals. As we navigate this dynamic landscape, understanding the nature of these threats is essential for safeguarding our digital future.

Chapter 2: Advanced Malware Classification and Analysis

Next, let's explore the fascinating realm of behavioral analysis and dynamic analysis in the context of cybersecurity.

In the ever-evolving battle against malware and cyber threats, it's crucial to employ diverse and sophisticated techniques for analysis and detection. Behavioral analysis and dynamic analysis are two such approaches that play pivotal roles in identifying and understanding the behavior of malicious software.

Behavioral analysis involves observing how a program behaves when it runs, without necessarily examining its underlying code. Think of it as monitoring the actions of a program as it interacts with a computer system. This technique is particularly valuable when dealing with previously unknown or "zero-day" threats, as it doesn't rely on specific signatures or patterns.

When a file or program is executed within a controlled environment, behavioral analysis observes its actions, such as file system changes, registry modifications, network communications, and system processes it spawns. By analyzing these behaviors, security analysts can detect suspicious or malicious activity. For instance, if a seemingly harmless program suddenly attempts to modify system files or establish unauthorized network connections, it raises red flags.

Dynamic analysis takes behavioral analysis a step further by executing the malware in a controlled environment known as a sandbox. A sandbox is a secure and isolated space where a file or program can run without posing a threat to the actual system. This controlled execution environment allows analysts to closely monitor the malware's behavior, capturing detailed information about its activities.

As the malware runs in the sandbox, dynamic analysis tools record its every move, from file changes to system calls, network traffic, and memory operations. This wealth of data is then analyzed to uncover its intentions and potential harm.

Dynamic analysis provides several advantages. It can reveal how a malware sample tries to evade detection, whether it exhibits polymorphic behavior (changing its code on each execution), and how it communicates with command and control servers. Analysts can even extract indicators of compromise (IOCs) from the dynamic analysis, which are valuable for future threat detection.

One key aspect of dynamic analysis is the ability to observe the malware's response to various stimuli. Analysts can manipulate the environment by introducing decoy files, simulated vulnerabilities, or other traps to gauge how the malware reacts. This interactive approach helps uncover hidden features, vulnerabilities it may attempt to exploit, or propagation methods it employs.

However, both behavioral and dynamic analysis have their limitations. Sophisticated malware often detects when it's running in a controlled environment, altering its behavior to appear benign. This behavior, known as sandbox evasion, is a cat-and-mouse game between attackers and defenders.

To overcome these challenges, cybersecurity professionals continuously improve dynamic analysis techniques. They employ a combination of multiple sandboxes, emulate a variety of environments, and implement advanced evasion detection methods to stay one step ahead of cyber adversaries.

Moreover, machine learning and artificial intelligence are playing increasingly prominent roles in behavioral and dynamic analysis. These technologies can automatically identify abnormal behavior patterns, enabling faster and more accurate threat detection.

In today's cybersecurity landscape, where the volume and complexity of threats continue to grow, behavioral and dynamic analysis are indispensable tools. They allow security experts to gain insights into the actions and intentions of malware, enabling them to respond swiftly and effectively to protect systems and data.

While these techniques are powerful, they are most effective when integrated into a broader cybersecurity strategy that includes signature-based detection, network monitoring, and user awareness training. The synergy of these elements creates a robust defense against an array of threats, both known and unknown.

As we continue to navigate the intricate world of cybersecurity, it's clear that behavioral and dynamic analysis will remain at the forefront of our efforts to combat malware and cyberattacks. By understanding how these techniques work and their significance in our digital lives, we empower ourselves to better safeguard our systems and data from evolving threats.

Next, let's delve into the intriguing world of heuristic and machine learning-based classification methods in the realm of cybersecurity.

In the ever-evolving landscape of cyber threats, the need for advanced techniques to identify and classify malicious software has become paramount. Heuristic analysis, coupled with machine learning, has emerged as a formidable duo in the battle against malware and other cyber adversaries.

Heuristic analysis, at its core, is a rule-based approach that relies on predefined algorithms and heuristics to identify potentially malicious behavior or attributes within a program or file. It's like having a set of guidelines or rules that help security systems make informed decisions about the nature of a file or program.

When a file or piece of code is subjected to heuristic analysis, the security system assesses various attributes, such as file size, file type, code obfuscation techniques, and known patterns of malicious behavior. If the analysis raises a sufficient number of red flags based on these predefined rules, the file is flagged as potentially malicious and subjected to further scrutiny.

Heuristic analysis is particularly valuable for identifying previously unknown or "zero-day" threats. Since it doesn't rely on known signatures or patterns, it can detect emerging threats that haven't yet been cataloged in antivirus databases. This proactive approach to threat detection is crucial in an environment where cybercriminals constantly create new variants of malware to evade detection.

However, heuristic analysis does have its limitations. False positives can occur when legitimate programs exhibit behavior that triggers heuristic rules, leading to the erroneous classification of safe files as malicious. To mitigate this, security analysts continually refine and update heuristic rules to strike a balance between accuracy and false positives.

This is where machine learning comes into play. Machine learning algorithms are designed to recognize patterns and make predictions based on data. In the context of cybersecurity, machine learning models can be trained on vast datasets of known malware and benign files to develop the ability to distinguish between the two.

Machine learning models can analyze a multitude of features extracted from files or code, such as byte sequences, API calls, and file metadata. By learning from historical data, these models can identify subtle, non-obvious patterns that may not be apparent through heuristic analysis alone. This capability makes machine learning-based classification highly effective in detecting both known and unknown threats.

One of the key advantages of machine learning is its adaptability. As cyber threats evolve, machine learning models can continuously learn and adapt to new attack techniques. They can even identify previously unseen malware variants by recognizing similarities to known malicious behaviors.

While heuristic analysis and machine learning-based classification are powerful tools in the cybersecurity arsenal, they are most effective when used in conjunction with other security measures. This multi-layered approach, often referred to as defense-in-depth, includes techniques like signature-based detection, network monitoring, and user awareness training.

Moreover, as machine learning continues to advance, we are witnessing the integration of artificial intelligence (AI) into cybersecurity. AI-driven solutions can autonomously analyze vast datasets, correlate complex patterns of behavior, and identify anomalies in real-time. This real-time threat detection capability is invaluable in today's rapidly changing threat landscape.

In summary, the combination of heuristic analysis and machine learning-based classification represents a critical advancement in our ability to identify and respond to cyber threats. These techniques enable security professionals to proactively defend against a wide range of malicious software, from well-known malware strains to previously unknown and sophisticated threats.

As we continue to explore the evolving field of cybersecurity, it's evident that heuristic analysis and machine learning-based classification are pivotal components of our defense strategy. By harnessing the power of these technologies, we are better equipped to protect our digital assets and stay ahead in the ongoing battle against cyber adversaries.

Chapter 3: Digital Forensics Techniques and Methodology

Next, let's delve into the crucial topic of acquiring and preserving digital evidence in the realm of digital forensics and cybersecurity.

In today's increasingly digitized world, digital evidence plays a pivotal role in investigations related to cybercrimes, data breaches, and other digital misconduct. This evidence can be the key to uncovering the truth and holding wrongdoers accountable, making the acquisition and preservation of digital evidence a critical part of the investigative process.

When we talk about the acquisition of digital evidence, we're referring to the process of collecting data from various digital sources, such as computers, mobile devices, servers, and cloud storage. The goal is to capture a snapshot of the system or device's state at a specific point in time, preserving the data in a forensically sound manner to ensure its admissibility in court.

The first step in this process involves identifying and securing the digital evidence. Investigators must take care to prevent any alterations, deletions, or unauthorized access to the data. This is often achieved by physically isolating the device or using specialized forensic tools to create a bit-by-bit copy, known as a forensic image, of the storage media.

Once the data is secured, it's crucial to document the acquisition process meticulously. This documentation includes details such as the date and time of acquisition, the individuals involved, and the tools and methods used. This documentation is essential to establish the chain of custody, which is a crucial element in ensuring the integrity of the evidence.

Digital evidence can take various forms, including files, emails, logs, and even network traffic. Each type of evidence requires specific techniques and tools for proper acquisition. For example, acquiring data from a desktop computer may involve creating a forensic image of the hard drive, while acquiring network traffic data may require capturing and preserving packets using specialized hardware or software.

Preserving digital evidence goes hand in hand with its acquisition. Preservation involves safeguarding the integrity of the acquired data to ensure that it remains unaltered and admissible in court. This means protecting the evidence from physical damage, electronic interference, or unauthorized access.

In many cases, digital evidence must be stored in a secure, controlled environment to prevent tampering or degradation. This may involve storing physical devices, such as hard drives or smartphones, in evidence lockers or using secure digital storage solutions that include encryption and access controls.

Furthermore, preserving digital evidence extends to ensuring its authenticity and reliability. Hash values, which are unique alphanumeric strings generated by applying cryptographic algorithms to data, play a vital role in verifying the integrity of digital evidence. By comparing the hash value of the original data with that of the acquired evidence, investigators can confirm that the evidence remains unchanged.

Another aspect of preservation involves maintaining a proper chain of custody. This is a documented record of everyone who has had contact with the evidence, from its acquisition to its presentation in court. Chain of custody records establish the continuity of possession and control of the evidence, demonstrating that it has not been tampered with or altered.

The handling of digital evidence requires a deep understanding of legal and ethical considerations. Investigators must be aware of privacy laws, data protection regulations, and the rights of individuals involved in the investigation. Adhering to established protocols and maintaining the highest ethical standards is essential to ensure that the evidence stands up to legal scrutiny.

In addition to acquisition and preservation, the analysis of digital evidence is a crucial step in any investigation. This analysis involves examining the data to extract relevant information, uncover patterns, and draw conclusions. Digital forensics tools and techniques, such as keyword searches, file recovery, and timeline analysis, are employed to assist in this process.

It's important to note that digital evidence can be fragile. Even seemingly minor actions, such as powering on a device or running a program, can alter or destroy critical evidence. Therefore, forensic experts must exercise extreme caution and follow established procedures to prevent any unintentional changes to the data.

In summary, the acquisition and preservation of digital evidence are fundamental aspects of modern investigative processes in cybersecurity and digital forensics. These practices ensure that evidence is collected and safeguarded in a way that maintains its integrity and admissibility in legal proceedings. By adhering to best practices, investigators can effectively uncover the truth and hold wrongdoers accountable in the ever-evolving digital landscape.

Now, let's explore the critical topic of the chain of custody and its intricate relationship with legal considerations in the realm of digital forensics and cybersecurity investigations.

The chain of custody, often abbreviated as CoC, is a meticulous and well-documented record of the chronological history of a piece of evidence from the moment it is collected until its presentation in a court of law or any other legal proceeding. Think of it as a trail of custody that ensures the evidence's integrity and admissibility.

Maintaining a robust chain of custody is of paramount importance in the world of digital forensics and cybersecurity investigations, where digital evidence serves as a cornerstone for identifying cybercriminals, proving their guilt, and securing convictions. The chain of custody begins the moment evidence is collected, whether it's a seized hard drive, a USB stick, or a network traffic capture.

This record provides a detailed account of every individual who comes into contact with the evidence, and it should include their names, roles, contact information, and the dates and times of their interactions. Furthermore, it should outline the locations where the evidence is stored, the conditions under which it is stored, and any transfers or movements.

One might wonder why such meticulous documentation is necessary. Well, the chain of custody serves several vital functions. Firstly, it ensures that evidence remains unaltered and trustworthy throughout the investigation process. Without a secure and documented chain of custody, defense attorneys could argue that evidence has been tampered with, potentially leading to its exclusion in court.

Secondly, the chain of custody establishes the continuity of possession and control over the evidence. This is critical for maintaining the reliability of the evidence, as it demonstrates that it has been in the custody of authorized personnel at all times.

Legal considerations play a central role in the management of the chain of custody. Understanding and adhering to relevant laws, regulations, and legal procedures is imperative for ensuring that digital evidence remains admissible in court.

Privacy laws, data protection regulations, and individuals' rights must be respected throughout the entire process. This means that investigators must take care not to infringe on the privacy of individuals whose data may be contained in the evidence. This can be especially complex in cross-border investigations where different jurisdictions have varying privacy laws.

Moreover, investigators must be aware of potential Fourth Amendment issues, which pertain to unreasonable searches and seizures. This is particularly relevant when dealing with evidence collected from individuals or organizations without their consent. In such cases, investigators must secure proper legal authorization, such as a search warrant or subpoena, to collect the evidence.

Additionally, investigators should be well-versed in the rules of evidence, which can vary depending on the jurisdiction and type of legal proceeding. They must ensure that the evidence they collect complies with the rules of relevance, admissibility, and authenticity set forth by the legal system.

Ethical considerations are intertwined with legal ones. While it may be legally permissible to collect certain evidence, it may not always be ethically sound. Digital forensics professionals should adhere to a strong code of ethics, placing the highest priority on honesty, integrity, and professionalism throughout the investigative process.

Furthermore, investigators should maintain transparency and open communication with all parties involved, including clients, legal teams, and law enforcement agencies. This helps to ensure that everyone understands the process and can provide input when necessary.

It's worth noting that the chain of custody doesn't end when the investigation concludes. Even after the evidence has been presented in court, its continued preservation and documentation may be required for potential appeals or future legal proceedings.

In summary, the chain of custody is a meticulous and well-documented record of a piece of evidence's journey from collection to courtroom presentation. It plays a pivotal role in preserving the integrity and admissibility of digital evidence in legal proceedings. By adhering to legal and ethical considerations, investigators can navigate the complexities of the chain of custody, ensuring that justice is served in the ever-evolving landscape of digital forensics and cybersecurity.

Chapter 4: Leveraging Advanced Analysis Tools

In today's rapidly evolving digital landscape, the sheer volume and complexity of malware strains pose an unprecedented challenge to cybersecurity professionals. Threat actors constantly develop new and sophisticated malware to compromise systems, steal data, and disrupt operations. To effectively combat this threat, security experts have turned to automated malware analysis platforms as indispensable tools in their arsenal. Automated malware analysis platforms, often referred to as sandboxes, represent a pivotal advancement in the battle against malware. These platforms are designed to mimic real computing environments, allowing security professionals to safely execute and analyze suspicious files or code without risking their actual systems. Think of them as virtual laboratories where digital forensics experts and cybersecurity analysts can dissect and study malware specimens in a controlled and secure manner.

The primary objective of automated malware analysis platforms is to uncover the inner workings of malicious software, understand its behavior, and extract critical information. They do this by employing a wide range of techniques and technologies, all automated and orchestrated to ensure efficiency and accuracy.

One of the fundamental capabilities of these platforms is dynamic analysis. Dynamic analysis involves executing malware in a controlled environment and monitoring its behavior in real-time. The platform records every action the malware takes, from file system changes to registry modifications, network communications, and system calls. Analysts can then examine this comprehensive behavioral data to identify malicious activities, such as attempts to exfiltrate sensitive data or establish unauthorized network connections.

Moreover, automated malware analysis platforms use signature-based detection techniques to identify known malware strains. They maintain extensive databases of malware signatures, which are unique identifiers or patterns of code associated with specific malware variants. When a suspicious file is analyzed, the platform cross-references it against these signatures to identify any matches, thus quickly detecting well-known threats. In addition to dynamic analysis and signature-based detection, these platforms often incorporate static analysis techniques. Static analysis involves examining the code and structure of a malware sample without executing it. Analysts can dissect the code to identify potential vulnerabilities, malicious functions, or obfuscation techniques used by the malware. This insight is invaluable for understanding how the malware operates and for developing effective countermeasures. Behavioral analysis is another critical component of automated malware analysis. This technique involves creating behavioral profiles for various malware families. By comparing the behavior of an analyzed sample to these profiles, analysts can gain insights into its characteristics and attributes. For instance, a malware sample may exhibit behavior consistent with ransomware, which encrypts files and demands a ransom for decryption keys. Furthermore, automated malware analysis platforms often provide detailed reports summarizing their findings. These reports include information about the malware's behavior, its potential impact on systems, and recommendations for remediation. This information is essential for cybersecurity teams to make informed decisions about how to respond to a malware incident effectively.

One notable advantage of automated malware analysis platforms is their scalability. In today's cyber landscape, the volume of malware samples that organizations encounter can be overwhelming. Automated platforms can process a large number of samples simultaneously, allowing security teams to quickly assess potential threats and prioritize their responses. Moreover, these platforms often integrate with other security solutions, creating a comprehensive cybersecurity ecosystem. They can feed data and intelligence into intrusion detection systems, threat intelligence platforms, and security information and event management (SIEM) systems, enhancing an organization's overall threat detection and response capabilities. However, it's important to note that automated malware analysis is not a panacea. While it is highly effective at identifying known malware and providing behavioral insights, it may struggle with highly sophisticated, zero-day threats that have not been previously documented. Threat actors continuously evolve their tactics to evade detection, making it essential for organizations to employ multiple layers of defense, including human expertise and threat intelligence, in conjunction with automated solutions. In summary, automated malware analysis platforms are indispensable tools in the battle against the ever-growing threat of malware. They provide organizations with the ability to efficiently and safely analyze and understand malicious software, helping to protect systems, data, and networks from cyber threats. As malware continues to evolve, so too will the capabilities of these platforms, enabling cybersecurity professionals to stay one step ahead of threat actors in our ongoing cybersecurity journey.

Imagine threat intelligence feeds as a constant stream of information about potential cyber threats and vulnerabilities. These feeds provide real-time updates on the latest malware strains, attack techniques, vulnerabilities, and even insights into the activities of threat actors and hacking groups. By incorporating these feeds into your cybersecurity infrastructure, you empower your organization to proactively identify, mitigate, and respond to threats effectively.

The concept of threat intelligence is akin to a neighborhood watch program in the digital realm. Just as a community shares information about suspicious activities and emerging threats to enhance security, threat intelligence feeds allow organizations to share and receive valuable data to strengthen their defenses. These feeds are collected from various sources, including government agencies, security vendors, open-source communities, and other trusted entities.

One primary benefit of integrating threat intelligence feeds is early threat detection. In the ever-escalating cat-and-mouse game between cybercriminals and defenders, staying ahead of threats is crucial. Threat intelligence feeds provide indicators of compromise (IOCs), such as malicious IP addresses, domain names, and file hashes, that can be used to detect ongoing or imminent attacks. By continually monitoring these indicators, organizations can spot threats in their infancy and respond before significant damage occurs.

Moreover, threat intelligence feeds offer valuable context. Instead of just knowing that a particular IP address is associated with malicious activity, organizations can gain insights into the tactics, techniques, and procedures (TTPs) of threat actors using that IP. This contextual information allows security teams to understand the bigger picture, identify potential attack vectors, and adapt their defenses accordingly. However, it's not just about early detection and contextual information; threat intelligence feeds also enable organizations to prioritize threats effectively. Not all threats are created equal, and not every indicator warrants the same level of attention. Threat intelligence feeds provide a risk assessment that helps organizations allocate their resources wisely. They can focus on high-risk indicators that pose a significant threat to their specific environment, ensuring a more efficient use of time and effort.

Incorporating threat intelligence feeds into your cybersecurity strategy involves a multifaceted approach. It begins with data collection, where organizations gather information from various sources. These sources can include government agencies, industry-specific organizations, commercial threat intelligence providers, and open-source feeds. By aggregating data from diverse sources, organizations gain a more comprehensive understanding of the threat landscape.

Next, the collected data needs to be processed and analyzed. This step involves filtering out noise and irrelevant information, ensuring that the intelligence is accurate and actionable. Automated tools and platforms can assist in this process, helping organizations extract valuable insights from the vast amounts of raw data they receive. Once the threat intelligence is processed and analyzed, it's crucial to disseminate this information to relevant stakeholders within the organization. This can include the security team, IT personnel, and even executives who need to be aware of potential risks. Timeliness is of the essence here, as actionable threat intelligence loses value if not acted upon promptly. To fully benefit from threat intelligence feeds, organizations should integrate this information into their security infrastructure. This means configuring security tools to automatically consume threat intelligence and use it to enhance detection and response capabilities. For example, a next-generation firewall can use threat intelligence to block traffic to known malicious IP addresses, while a SIEM system can correlate threat intelligence data with internal logs to identify anomalies and potential security incidents.

Collaboration is a key aspect of threat intelligence. Organizations should consider sharing their own threat intelligence with trusted partners and information-sharing communities. In a collective effort to combat cyber threats, sharing insights about emerging threats and attack techniques strengthens the overall security posture. Moreover, threat intelligence feeds should be part of an organization's incident response plan. By incorporating threat intelligence into incident detection and response processes, organizations can rapidly identify and contain threats. For example, when an indicator of compromise is detected, the incident response team can use threat intelligence to understand the nature of the threat and take appropriate action. However, it's essential to recognize that threat intelligence is not a one-size-fits-all solution. Organizations must tailor their use of threat intelligence to their specific needs and risk profile. This means understanding the industry-specific threats they face, the types of data they need to protect, and the regulatory requirements they must adhere to.

In summary, incorporating threat intelligence feeds into your cybersecurity strategy is more critical than ever in our interconnected digital world. These feeds provide real-time, contextualized, and actionable information that empowers organizations to proactively defend against cyber threats. By following a comprehensive approach to collecting, processing, disseminating, and integrating threat intelligence, organizations can enhance their security posture and stay ahead of evolving threats.

Chapter 5: Memory Forensics and Artifact Extraction

In the intricate world of digital forensics and incident response, the examination of RAM, or Random Access Memory, holds a crucial role in uncovering valuable artifacts that can shed light on past activities and security incidents. RAM, the volatile memory of a computer, is a temporary storage location for data actively used by running processes and applications. It's like the workspace where the computer's brain performs its tasks. This workspace is dynamic, ever-changing, and, most importantly, transient.

When it comes to identifying and extracting artifacts from RAM, it's essential to understand the significance of this process. RAM contains a wealth of information about the current state of a system, but it also retains traces of past activities. These traces can be invaluable for digital forensics and incident response professionals when investigating security incidents, uncovering malware infections, or identifying malicious activity.

Now, let's delve into the nitty-gritty of how this process works. RAM forensics involves capturing the contents of a computer's RAM at a specific point in time and then analyzing this captured data to identify relevant artifacts. The process typically starts with acquiring a memory dump, also known as a memory image, which is a snapshot of the entire RAM at a given moment. This can be done using various tools and techniques, including dedicated memory acquisition tools or by utilizing operating system functions.

Once the memory dump is acquired, the next step is to extract and analyze the artifacts. Artifacts in RAM can take many forms, including running processes, network connections, loaded dynamic link libraries (DLLs), open files, and more. These artifacts can provide insights into ongoing or past activities on the system.

One of the primary artifacts of interest is the list of running processes. Analyzing this list can help identify suspicious or malicious processes that may be running on the system. By examining the attributes of these processes, such as their file paths, command-line arguments, and associated parent processes, investigators can determine if any of them are related to a security incident.

Another critical artifact is the list of open network connections. This can reveal any network communication occurring at the time of the memory capture. Investigators can identify connections to known malicious IP addresses or domains, as well as the processes responsible for these connections. This information is vital for understanding potential data exfiltration or command-and-control activity.

Loaded DLLs, or dynamic link libraries, are also essential artifacts to examine. Malware often injects malicious code into the memory space of legitimate processes by loading malicious DLLs. Identifying these loaded DLLs can help investigators pinpoint instances of code injection and understand how malware is persisting on the system.

File handles and open files are another set of artifacts that can provide valuable insights. Investigators can identify files that were open at the time of the memory capture, helping to uncover any suspicious or unauthorized access to sensitive data.

Beyond these core artifacts, RAM forensics can reveal a wealth of additional information, such as user credentials, registry hives in memory, and evidence of volatile attacks like privilege escalation or process injection.

To perform this level of analysis effectively, digital forensics professionals rely on specialized tools and techniques. Memory analysis frameworks like Volatility and Rekall provide a range of plugins and capabilities for extracting and parsing memory artifacts. These tools can interpret memory structures, reconstruct data, and present it in a human-readable format.

When working with memory artifacts, it's essential to maintain the integrity of the captured data. Chain of custody procedures, similar to those used for physical evidence in a crime scene investigation, must be followed to ensure that the memory image is admissible in legal proceedings.

Moreover, investigators should also be aware of the limitations of RAM forensics. RAM is volatile, meaning that its contents are lost when the computer is powered down or restarted. Therefore, capturing a memory image must be done as soon as possible after the incident or while the system is still running to preserve critical evidence.

In summary, identifying and extracting artifacts from RAM is a vital component of digital forensics and incident response. This process allows investigators to uncover valuable insights into past activities and security incidents. By capturing a memory dump and carefully analyzing the artifacts within, professionals can piece together the puzzle of what transpired on a compromised system, identify malicious activity, and take appropriate remedial actions.

Memory-resident malware, a category of malicious software that resides solely in a computer's volatile memory (RAM), presents a unique and challenging threat to cybersecurity professionals and digital forensics experts. Unlike traditional malware that resides on disk drives, memory-resident malware operates in the ephemeral space of RAM, making it elusive, difficult to detect, and particularly pernicious.

To effectively analyze memory-resident malware components, one must first grasp the fundamental characteristics of this type of threat. Memory-resident malware is designed to execute directly from RAM, without leaving traces on a computer's storage devices. This evasive behavior enables it to avoid detection by traditional antivirus and antimalware tools that primarily focus on scanning files stored on disk.

One common example of memory-resident malware is known as a "RAM scraper." These types of malware are often used in credit card data theft attacks on point-of-sale (POS) systems. RAM scrapers target the computer's memory, where sensitive data, such as credit card numbers, is briefly stored during transactions. By residing in memory, the malware can intercept and capture this data in real-time without ever writing it to disk, thus avoiding detection by signature-based antivirus solutions.

To analyze memory-resident malware components effectively, one must employ specialized techniques and tools designed for this purpose. Traditional static analysis methods, which involve examining the code or binary of a malware sample on disk, are not applicable in this context since memory-resident malware does not persist on disk. Instead, analysts rely on dynamic analysis, which involves observing the malware's behavior while it is actively running in memory.

Memory analysis tools, like Volatility and Rekall, play a pivotal role in this process. These tools allow analysts to capture a snapshot of the computer's RAM at a particular point in time, creating a memory dump or image. This memory image can then be analyzed to identify and dissect memory-resident malware components.

One key objective of memory analysis is to locate and isolate the malicious code within memory. Memory-resident malware typically injects its code into legitimate processes or creates its own processes in memory. Identifying these injected or newly created processes is the first step in understanding the malware's behavior.

Another critical aspect of memory analysis is identifying indicators of compromise (IOCs). IOCs are specific artifacts or patterns of behavior that indicate the presence of malware. In memory analysis, IOCs may include unusual or suspicious network connections, registry modifications, code injection techniques, and the presence of known malicious code patterns.

In addition to identifying IOCs, analysts must reconstruct the malware's execution flow. This involves tracing the sequence of instructions executed by the malware within the memory space. This step helps analysts understand the malware's capabilities, such as its ability to steal data, communicate with command-and-control servers, or propagate within a network.

Memory-resident malware often employs anti-analysis and evasion techniques to thwart detection and analysis. These techniques can include encryption of its code and data, polymorphic code that changes its appearance with each execution, and rootkit functionality to hide its presence. Analysts must be well-versed in countering these evasion tactics to successfully analyze memory-resident malware.

Furthermore, to analyze memory-resident malware effectively, it's crucial to consider the context in which it operates. Understanding the broader attack scenario, including how the malware was initially delivered to the system and the goals of the threat actor, can provide valuable insights into the incident. This holistic approach to analysis is essential for developing a comprehensive understanding of the threat.

In many cases, memory-resident malware is part of a larger attack campaign. By analyzing the malware's components and behavior, cybersecurity professionals can uncover the tactics, techniques, and procedures (TTPs) employed by threat actors. This knowledge can inform incident response efforts and help organizations strengthen their security posture to prevent future attacks.

In summary, the analysis of memory-resident malware components is a specialized and critical skill in the field of cybersecurity and digital forensics. Memory-resident malware presents unique challenges due to its volatile nature and evasive behavior. To effectively analyze and respond to these threats, professionals must rely on dynamic memory analysis techniques, specialized tools, and a deep understanding of malware behavior. By successfully dissecting memory-resident malware, organizations can mitigate the risks posed by these elusive adversaries and protect their digital assets.

Chapter 6: Network Traffic Analysis and Intrusion Detection

Deep Packet Inspection (DPI) is a sophisticated network analysis technique that plays a pivotal role in modern cybersecurity and threat detection efforts. At its core, DPI is a method of inspecting and analyzing the contents of data packets as they traverse a network. It enables security professionals to gain deep insights into network traffic, identify potential threats, and respond proactively to cyberattacks.

In the ever-evolving landscape of cyber threats, traditional network security measures, such as firewalls and intrusion detection systems (IDS), have become less effective in detecting and mitigating sophisticated attacks. Cybercriminals continually refine their tactics, techniques, and procedures (TTPs), making it essential for defenders to have advanced tools like DPI at their disposal.

DPI operates at the packet level, which means it scrutinizes the actual data within network packets, including the payload, headers, and even metadata. Unlike conventional firewall rules that rely on port and protocol information, DPI goes much deeper, examining the actual content of packets to understand the nature of the data being transmitted.

One of the primary applications of DPI is in the detection of network-based threats, such as malware, viruses, and intrusion attempts. By analyzing the content of network packets, DPI can identify patterns or signatures associated with known threats. This allows security teams to recognize and block malicious traffic in real-time, preventing cyberattacks before they can penetrate a network.

Furthermore, DPI can play a crucial role in identifying and mitigating advanced persistent threats (APTs). APTs are sophisticated, stealthy attacks often orchestrated by nation-state actors or well-funded cybercriminal organizations. These threats typically involve multiple stages and employ various evasion techniques to avoid detection. DPI's ability to scrutinize packet contents allows it to uncover subtle indicators of compromise (IOCs) that may be indicative of an ongoing APT.

One of the key advantages of DPI is its ability to perform content-based filtering. This means that security policies can be crafted to filter out specific content or keywords within network traffic. For example, an organization might use DPI to block the transmission of sensitive data, such as credit card numbers or personally identifiable information (PII), to prevent data breaches.

Additionally, DPI is invaluable for monitoring and enforcing compliance with acceptable use policies. By inspecting the content of packets, organizations can detect and prevent the unauthorized use of applications or services that may pose security risks or violate corporate policies. This includes identifying employees who are using unauthorized messaging or file-sharing applications that could potentially expose the organization to data leaks or malware infections.

Intrusion detection and prevention systems (IDPS) often leverage DPI to enhance their capabilities. These systems rely on DPI to identify and block suspicious or malicious network traffic patterns, providing an additional layer of defense against cyber threats. DPI enables IDPS to look beyond simple packet header information and evaluate the actual content for signs of malicious activity.

It's worth noting that DPI is not limited to threat detection alone. It also plays a vital role in traffic optimization and quality of service (QoS) management. By analyzing the contents of packets, network administrators can prioritize critical applications or services, ensuring that they receive adequate bandwidth and minimizing network congestion.

In practice, DPI is implemented through specialized hardware or software appliances, commonly referred to as DPI engines or DPI devices. These devices are strategically placed within a network's infrastructure to inspect traffic as it flows through. DPI engines use a combination of signature-based detection, heuristic analysis, and anomaly detection techniques to identify potential threats.

However, it's important to recognize that DPI also raises concerns related to user privacy and network neutrality. The deep inspection of packet contents raises questions about data privacy and the potential for network operators or security teams to monitor and analyze user communications. Striking a balance between security and privacy is a challenge that organizations must navigate when implementing DPI.

In summary, Deep Packet Inspection is a powerful tool in the arsenal of cybersecurity professionals and network administrators. Its ability to analyze the actual content of network packets enables organizations to detect and mitigate a wide range of threats, from malware and APTs to data breaches and policy violations. While DPI offers substantial security benefits, it also raises important considerations related to privacy and ethical use, emphasizing the need for responsible and transparent implementation. In an era of ever-evolving cyber threats, Deep Packet Inspection stands as a critical defense mechanism in safeguarding digital assets and data integrity.

Intrusion Detection Systems (IDS) are vital components of modern cybersecurity strategies, serving as the front lines of defense against a barrage of cyber threats. To harness the full potential of an IDS and ensure its effectiveness in safeguarding your organization's digital assets, it's crucial to adhere to a set of best practices.

Understanding Your Network Environment: Before implementing an IDS, it's essential to have a comprehensive understanding of your network environment. This includes identifying critical assets, network topologies, traffic patterns, and potential vulnerabilities. This knowledge will help you tailor your IDS to the specific needs and risks of your organization.

Strategic Placement of Sensors: Proper placement of IDS sensors is pivotal. Sensors should be strategically located at key points within your network, such as at ingress and egress points, in demilitarized zones (DMZs), and close to critical assets. This ensures comprehensive coverage and the ability to detect threats as they traverse the network.

Choosing the Right IDS Type: Selecting the appropriate type of IDS is essential. Network-based IDS (NIDS) monitors network traffic, while host-based IDS (HIDS) focuses on individual systems. Depending on your organization's needs, you may choose to deploy both NIDS and HIDS for a layered approach to security.

Regular Signature Updates: Keep your IDS signatures up to date. Signatures are patterns that IDS systems use to identify known threats. Cyber threats evolve constantly, so regularly updating signatures is essential for detecting new threats effectively.

Tuning and Customization: Customize your IDS to reduce false positives and focus on the most relevant threats. Fine-tuning your IDS involves configuring it to match the specific characteristics of your network, which can help you avoid unnecessary alerts.

Monitoring and Alerting: Establish a robust monitoring and alerting process. Ensure that your IDS generates alerts for suspicious activities and that these alerts are reviewed by security personnel. Prompt responses to alerts are critical in preventing potential breaches.

Incident Response Integration: Integrate your IDS with your incident response plan. When your IDS generates alerts, it should trigger predefined actions within your incident response framework, streamlining the process of containing and mitigating threats.

Regular Testing and Evaluation: Regularly test and evaluate your IDS. Conduct penetration tests and simulate attacks to assess how effectively your IDS can detect and respond to threats. Regular testing helps identify weaknesses and areas for improvement.

User Training: Train your IT and security teams on how to use the IDS effectively. Ensure that your personnel can interpret alerts, understand the IDS's capabilities, and respond appropriately to security incidents.

Continuous Monitoring: Intrusion detection is an ongoing process. Implement continuous monitoring to keep a vigilant eye on your network. Continuous monitoring allows for the timely detection of new threats and vulnerabilities.

Log Analysis: Integrate your IDS with log analysis tools. Analyzing logs generated by your IDS can provide valuable insights into network activities and help identify potential threats that might not trigger traditional IDS alerts.

Threat Intelligence Integration: Incorporate threat intelligence feeds into your IDS. Threat intelligence provides real-time information about emerging threats and known attack patterns, enhancing the ability of your IDS to detect and respond to the latest threats.

Documentation and Reporting: Maintain comprehensive documentation of your IDS configuration, policies, and procedures. Clear documentation ensures that all team members understand how the IDS functions and enables effective reporting to stakeholders.

Scalability: Plan for scalability. As your organization grows, your network and security requirements will evolve. Ensure that your IDS can scale to meet future demands without compromising performance.

Compliance Considerations: Align your IDS implementation with industry-specific regulations and compliance standards. Compliance requirements often dictate the need for specific IDS configurations and reporting capabilities.

Collaboration with Other Security Solutions: Integrate your IDS with other security solutions, such as firewalls, antivirus software, and security information and event management (SIEM) systems. Collaborative security tools create a unified defense strategy.

Monitoring for False Negatives: Don't solely focus on false positives. Be vigilant in monitoring for false negatives, which are instances where the IDS fails to detect actual threats. Regularly review and refine your IDS policies to minimize false negatives.

Regular Review and Updates: Security threats and network environments evolve. Regularly review and update your IDS policies, configurations, and hardware to stay aligned with the changing threat landscape.

In summary, effective Intrusion Detection System (IDS) implementation and management require a holistic approach. By understanding your network, strategically deploying sensors, staying up to date, customizing your IDS, and integrating it into your broader security infrastructure, you can enhance your organization's ability to detect and respond to cyber threats effectively. Additionally, a strong emphasis on training, documentation, and compliance ensures that your IDS is a valuable asset in your cybersecurity toolkit.

Chapter 7: Threat Intelligence Integration

Leveraging threat intelligence feeds is a fundamental practice in modern cybersecurity that empowers organizations to stay one step ahead of cyber threats. Threat intelligence feeds provide organizations with real-time information about emerging threats, vulnerabilities, and malicious actors, enabling them to make informed decisions and bolster their defenses. In this chapter, we will explore the significance of threat intelligence feeds, their types, sources, and how organizations can effectively utilize this invaluable resource.

To begin with, threat intelligence feeds are a valuable source of information that helps organizations proactively identify and respond to cyber threats. These feeds aggregate data from various sources, including government agencies, security researchers, cybersecurity vendors, open-source projects, and dark web forums, among others. This diverse range of sources ensures that organizations receive a comprehensive view of the threat landscape.

One of the primary benefits of leveraging threat intelligence feeds is their ability to provide early warnings about potential threats. By monitoring these feeds, organizations can gain insights into new vulnerabilities, malware strains, attack techniques, and indicators of compromise (IOCs) as they emerge. This early warning system allows organizations to take proactive measures to protect their systems and data.

Threat intelligence feeds come in various types, each serving specific purposes. These types include strategic, operational, and tactical intelligence feeds. Strategic feeds provide high-level information about global threat trends, helping organizations understand the broader cybersecurity landscape. Operational feeds offer more specific insights into ongoing threats and campaigns, while tactical feeds provide granular details about specific threats, such as malware samples and attack methods.

The sources of threat intelligence are equally diverse, encompassing both open and closed sources. Open sources include publicly available information, such as news reports, blogs, and social media. Closed sources, on the other hand, involve subscription-based services, information-sharing groups, and private threat intelligence vendors. A combination of open and closed sources provides organizations with a well-rounded understanding of the threat landscape.

To effectively leverage threat intelligence feeds, organizations must establish a structured process for collecting, analyzing, and operationalizing the intelligence. This process typically involves the following steps:

Collection: Gathering threat intelligence from various sources, both open and closed.

Normalization: Converting the collected data into a standardized format that can be easily processed and analyzed.

Enrichment: Enhancing the data with additional context, such as threat actor profiles, historical attack data, and attack patterns.

Analysis: Evaluating the threat intelligence for relevance and credibility, and assessing its potential impact on the organization.

Correlation: Identifying connections between different pieces of threat intelligence to uncover hidden patterns and relationships.

Prioritization: Assigning priority levels to threats based on their potential impact and relevance to the organization.

Distribution: Sharing threat intelligence with relevant stakeholders within the organization, such as security teams and incident responders.

Action: Taking proactive measures to mitigate threats, which may include updating security policies, deploying additional security controls, or implementing patches.

Feedback Loop: Continuously monitoring the effectiveness of threat intelligence in improving security posture and making adjustments as needed.

It's important to note that threat intelligence feeds are not a one-size-fits-all solution. Organizations should tailor their threat intelligence strategy to their specific needs and threat landscape. This customization involves selecting the most relevant feeds, defining alert thresholds, and integrating threat intelligence into existing security infrastructure.

Furthermore, threat intelligence feeds are most effective when integrated with security information and event management (SIEM) systems, intrusion detection systems (IDS), and security orchestration, automation, and response (SOAR) platforms. This integration allows for automated responses to threats and streamlines incident response processes.

In addition to their proactive benefits, threat intelligence feeds also play a crucial role in post-incident analysis and attribution. After a security incident, organizations can refer to threat intelligence feeds to identify the threat actor responsible, understand their tactics, techniques, and procedures (TTPs), and assess the potential impact on the organization.

However, leveraging threat intelligence feeds effectively comes with its challenges. One of the foremost challenges is the sheer volume of data generated by these feeds. Organizations must have the necessary infrastructure and tools to process and analyze large quantities of threat intelligence data efficiently. Moreover, organizations should be cautious of false positives and outdated information, which can lead to unnecessary alerts and wasted resources.

To address these challenges, organizations often employ threat intelligence platforms (TIPs) that provide a centralized hub for collecting, analyzing, and distributing threat intelligence. These platforms offer automation capabilities, threat scoring, and alerting mechanisms to help organizations sift through vast amounts of data and focus on the most critical threats.

In summary, leveraging threat intelligence feeds is a cornerstone of modern cybersecurity, empowering organizations to proactively defend against evolving cyber threats. By collecting, analyzing, and operationalizing threat intelligence, organizations can strengthen their security posture, respond effectively to incidents, and ultimately stay ahead of threat actors in the ever-changing cyber landscape. However, successful threat intelligence implementation requires a well-defined process, customization to organizational needs, integration with existing security tools, and a vigilant approach to managing the challenges associated with threat data volume and accuracy.

Developing effective incident response playbooks is a critical component of any organization's cybersecurity strategy, ensuring a structured and well-coordinated approach to handling security incidents. These playbooks serve as a set of predefined procedures and guidelines that help security teams respond promptly and efficiently when security incidents occur. In this chapter, we will delve into the significance of incident response playbooks, their key elements, and the steps involved in creating them.

Incident response playbooks are akin to well-rehearsed scripts for dealing with security incidents. They provide security teams with a clear roadmap for detecting, analyzing, mitigating, and recovering from various types of incidents, ranging from data breaches to malware infections and denial-of-service attacks. Having predefined playbooks in place reduces response time, minimizes human error, and ensures a consistent and coordinated response across the organization.

The creation of effective incident response playbooks begins with a deep understanding of an organization's unique threat landscape, its assets, and its tolerance for risk. To this end, organizations should start by conducting a comprehensive risk assessment and identifying the potential threats and vulnerabilities they face. This initial assessment serves as the foundation for tailoring incident response procedures to specific risks and scenarios.

Key elements that should be included in incident response playbooks encompass the following:

Roles and Responsibilities: Clearly define the roles and responsibilities of each team member involved in incident response. This includes designating incident handlers, communication leads, legal advisors, and any other relevant personnel.

Notification and Escalation Procedures: Establish guidelines for how incidents should be reported, who should be notified, and the criteria for escalating incidents to higher levels of management or external entities, such as law enforcement or regulatory bodies.

Incident Classification: Define a system for categorizing incidents based on their severity and impact. This classification helps in prioritizing incident response efforts and allocating resources effectively.

Data Collection and Preservation: Outline procedures for collecting and preserving evidence related to the incident. This includes guidelines for collecting logs, memory dumps, network traffic data, and any other relevant artifacts.

Technical Response Procedures: Specify the technical steps that should be taken to contain, mitigate, and eradicate the incident. These procedures may involve isolating affected systems, patching vulnerabilities, and removing malicious software.

Communication Plans: Develop communication plans for both internal and external stakeholders. This includes drafting templates for incident notifications, press releases, and updates to customers or partners.

Legal and Regulatory Compliance: Ensure that the incident response playbook aligns with legal and regulatory requirements specific to the organization's industry and jurisdiction.

Incident Recovery: Describe the steps required to recover from the incident, including system restoration, data recovery, and post-incident analysis.

Continuous Improvement: Emphasize the importance of post-incident debriefings and lessons learned. Encourage teams to document what worked well and what could be improved for future incidents.

Testing and Simulation: Incorporate regular testing and simulation exercises into the playbook to ensure that response procedures are effective and that team members are familiar with their roles.

Creating an incident response playbook involves several iterative steps:

Assessment and Planning: As mentioned earlier, begin with a thorough assessment of an organization's risk landscape. Identify potential threats, vulnerabilities, and assets that need protection.

Risk Analysis: Evaluate the potential impact and likelihood of different incidents. This analysis informs the prioritization of response efforts and resource allocation.

Development: With a clear understanding of risks and priorities, develop the playbook, outlining procedures and guidelines for each element mentioned earlier.

Review and Approval: Subject the playbook to a review process involving key stakeholders, including legal, IT, and executive teams. Ensure that all parties are aligned on the response procedures.

Testing and Validation: Conduct tabletop exercises and simulations to validate the playbook's effectiveness. Identify any gaps or areas that require refinement.

Training: Provide training to incident response teams and other relevant personnel to ensure they are well-prepared to execute the procedures outlined in the playbook.

Implementation: Put the playbook into action by making it readily accessible to incident response teams. Ensure that all team members are familiar with its content.

Continuous Improvement: Periodically review and update the playbook to account for changes in the threat landscape, regulatory requirements, or improvements in response procedures.

It's important to recognize that incident response playbooks should not be static documents. They should evolve alongside an organization's changing threat landscape and technological environment. Regularly reviewing and updating playbooks ensures that they remain relevant and effective in addressing emerging threats.

In addition, organizations should consider the integration of incident response playbooks with security orchestration, automation, and response (SOAR) platforms. These platforms can streamline incident response processes by automating certain tasks, orchestrating responses, and providing real-time visibility into ongoing incidents.

In summary, developing effective incident response playbooks is a fundamental aspect of a proactive cybersecurity strategy. These playbooks provide organizations with a structured and well-coordinated approach to handling security incidents, reducing response times, minimizing human error, and ensuring consistency across the organization. Creating playbooks involves a thorough assessment of an organization's risk landscape, the development of response procedures, regular testing and validation, and ongoing updates to adapt to evolving threats and technologies. With well-crafted playbooks in place, organizations are better equipped to protect their assets and respond effectively to the ever-changing cybersecurity landscape.

Chapter 8: Incident Response Playbooks and Automation

Automation plays a pivotal role in the realm of incident response, transforming the way organizations handle security incidents by enabling rapid and efficient responses. In this chapter, we will explore the significance of automation in incident response, the various aspects of automation, and how it empowers organizations to bolster their cybersecurity posture.

The advent of automation has ushered in a new era in the field of incident response, revolutionizing how organizations detect, analyze, and mitigate security threats. The relentless evolution of cyber threats, coupled with the sheer volume of incidents organizations face, demands a more agile and streamlined approach to incident response. Automation provides the means to achieve this agility.

One of the primary advantages of automation in incident response is its ability to expedite the detection of security incidents. Traditional manual methods of incident detection often involve sifting through vast amounts of logs and data, a time-consuming process that can delay response efforts significantly. Automation tools, on the other hand, can swiftly analyze and correlate data from multiple sources, flagging anomalies and potential threats in real-time. This accelerated detection capability is crucial in identifying and neutralizing threats before they escalate.

Automation also plays a critical role in incident triage and classification. When a potential security incident is detected, automation tools can assess the severity and relevance of the threat by comparing it to predefined criteria and threat intelligence feeds. This classification process enables organizations to prioritize incidents based on their potential impact and allocate resources accordingly. High-risk incidents can be escalated for immediate attention, while lower-priority incidents can be addressed in due course.

The rapid containment of security incidents is another area where automation excels. Once an incident is classified, automation tools can execute predefined response actions, such as isolating affected systems, blocking malicious traffic, or disabling compromised accounts. This automated containment mitigates the spread of threats and minimizes the damage inflicted by attackers. It also reduces the burden on incident response teams, allowing them to focus on more complex tasks.

Furthermore, automation facilitates the collection of forensic data and evidence, a crucial aspect of incident response. When an incident occurs, automated tools can initiate data collection procedures, including the preservation of system logs, memory snapshots, and network traffic data. This ensures that valuable evidence is secured for later analysis and potential legal proceedings, while minimizing the risk of data loss or tampering.

Effective incident response often requires collaboration among various teams within an organization, including IT, security, legal, and communications. Automation tools enable seamless coordination and communication among these teams by providing a centralized platform for incident management. Information about ongoing incidents, response progress, and key actions can be shared in real-time, ensuring that all stakeholders are well-informed and aligned in their efforts.

Another significant benefit of automation is its capacity for incident recovery and remediation. After an incident is contained and investigated, automated tools can assist in the process of restoring affected systems to their normal operational state. This may involve the deployment of patches, the removal of malicious software, and the validation of system integrity. Automated recovery procedures help organizations return to business as usual more swiftly, minimizing downtime and financial losses.

One of the critical aspects of automation in incident response is its adaptability to the evolving threat landscape. Cyber threats are continually changing, with attackers employing increasingly sophisticated techniques. Automation tools can be configured to stay updated with the latest threat intelligence feeds, ensuring that they can detect and respond to emerging threats effectively. This adaptability is crucial for organizations to maintain a proactive stance against cyber adversaries.

While automation offers numerous advantages in incident response, it is not without its challenges. Implementing automation requires careful planning and consideration. Organizations must define clear workflows, response procedures, and criteria for automation triggers. It's essential to strike a balance between automation and human intervention, as not all incidents can be addressed solely through automated processes.

Moreover, automation tools must be carefully chosen and integrated into an organization's existing security infrastructure. Compatibility and interoperability with other security solutions are critical to ensure a seamless and efficient incident response process. Additionally, organizations should invest in adequate training and skill development for their incident response teams to leverage automation effectively.

In summary, automation has become an indispensable component of modern incident response strategies. Its ability to expedite incident detection, triage, containment, and recovery, while adapting to the ever-evolving threat landscape, makes it a valuable ally in the fight against cyber threats. Organizations that embrace automation in their incident response workflows gain a competitive edge in safeguarding their digital assets and maintaining the trust of their stakeholders. As the cybersecurity landscape continues to evolve, the role of automation in incident response will undoubtedly become even more pronounced and essential.

In the complex realm of cybersecurity, one of the most challenging aspects is the identification of insider threats. These threats originate from within an organization, posing a significant risk to data security, intellectual property, and the overall integrity of an organization's operations. In this chapter, we'll delve into the various indicators that can help organizations identify insider threats and the importance of vigilance in safeguarding their digital assets.

Understanding the motivations behind insider threats is the first step in identifying potential indicators. Insider threats can be classified into three main categories: malicious insiders, negligent insiders, and compromised insiders. Malicious insiders intentionally engage in harmful activities, driven by personal gain, revenge, or ideology.

Negligent insiders, on the other hand, inadvertently compromise security due to carelessness or a lack of awareness. Compromised insiders are individuals whose credentials have been stolen or compromised by external threat actors, turning them into unwitting accomplices.

One of the most common indicators of malicious insiders is unusual or suspicious behavior patterns. Monitoring user activities, such as file access, system logins, and data transfers, can reveal deviations from established norms. Frequent access to sensitive data outside of job responsibilities, especially during non-working hours, can be a red flag. Similarly, attempts to bypass security controls, like disabling antivirus software or altering firewall rules, are indicators that warrant investigation.

Another indicator to consider is an abrupt change in an employee's work attitude or performance. Malicious insiders may exhibit signs of discontent, such as expressing grievances against the organization or colleagues. They might resist company policies and security measures or actively seek unauthorized access to sensitive information. A sudden decline in job performance can also indicate a disgruntled employee's intention to harm the organization.

Financial irregularities can serve as valuable indicators of insider threats. Unauthorized access to financial records, unusual transactions, or discrepancies in financial reports can be signs of insider wrongdoing. Employees with access to financial systems may exploit their privileges for personal gain, embezzlement, or fraud, making financial monitoring an essential aspect of insider threat detection.

In some cases, employees may engage in information hoarding, wherein they accumulate sensitive data beyond their job requirements. This behavior can be a precursor to data exfiltration, as the insider stockpiles information for potential misuse or unauthorized disclosure. Monitoring excessive downloading or copying of files can help identify this indicator.

Social indicators can also be revealing when it comes to insider threats. Changes in an employee's interpersonal relationships within the organization can signal potential issues. A sudden isolation from coworkers, disputes with colleagues, or a noticeable shift in allegiance and alliances can be indicative of underlying problems. Monitoring employee interactions and communication patterns can shed light on these social indicators.

To effectively identify insider threats, organizations should implement comprehensive user and entity behavior analytics (UEBA) systems. UEBA tools employ machine learning and advanced analytics to detect anomalous behaviors and patterns that may indicate insider threats. These systems analyze vast amounts of data from various sources, including user activities, network traffic, and endpoint devices, to identify subtle deviations from normal behavior.

In addition to technological solutions, establishing a culture of security awareness is crucial for detecting insider threats. Regular training programs can educate employees about the risks associated with insider threats, emphasizing the importance of reporting suspicious activities. Encouraging an open and transparent reporting environment ensures that employees feel comfortable raising concerns without fear of retribution.

When dealing with negligent insiders, continuous monitoring and auditing of user activities are paramount.

Proactive measures, such as implementing data loss prevention (DLP) solutions and access controls, can help mitigate the risks posed by employees who may inadvertently compromise security. Periodic security assessments and vulnerability scans can uncover potential weaknesses in an organization's defense mechanisms.

Compromised insider threats require a different approach. Organizations must focus on early detection by monitoring for unusual login patterns, unauthorized access attempts, and account behavior anomalies. Implementing multi-factor authentication (MFA) and robust password policies can reduce the likelihood of credential compromise.

In summary, the identification of insider threat indicators is a critical aspect of cybersecurity. By understanding the motivations and behaviors associated with malicious, negligent, and compromised insiders, organizations can take proactive measures to detect and mitigate these threats. Combining technology-driven solutions, such as UEBA and DLP, with a security-aware culture and ongoing employee training, is essential for safeguarding an organization's digital assets and maintaining trust in an ever-evolving threat landscape.

Chapter 9: Insider Threats and Advanced Adversary Detection

In the ever-evolving landscape of cybersecurity, the detection of adversaries who seek to infiltrate, compromise, or sabotage an organization's digital infrastructure has become a paramount concern. Traditional security measures are often inadequate against determined adversaries, necessitating the development and deployment of advanced techniques for adversary detection.

One of the primary challenges in adversary detection is the ability of sophisticated threat actors to blend seamlessly into an organization's network. Unlike more straightforward cyberattacks, which often leave conspicuous traces, advanced adversaries employ tactics, techniques, and procedures (TTPs) that mimic legitimate user behavior and traffic patterns. Detecting these subtle anomalies requires a multi-faceted and proactive approach.

Behavioral analysis stands as a cornerstone in advanced adversary detection. By continuously monitoring user and network activities, security teams can establish baselines of normal behavior. Deviations from these baselines, such as unusual access patterns, file transfers, or login attempts, may indicate the presence of an adversary. Behavioral analysis leverages machine learning algorithms to detect patterns of behavior that are inconsistent with the expected norms, thereby flagging potential threats.

Another advanced technique for adversary detection is the use of honeytokens and honeypots. Honeytokens are decoy files, credentials, or system resources intentionally placed within an organization's environment to attract adversaries. When these honeytokens are accessed or manipulated, it triggers an alert, revealing the presence of an intruder. Honeypots are entire systems or networks designed to lure adversaries away from critical assets. Analyzing interactions with these deceptive assets provides valuable insights into adversary behavior and intentions.

Continuous monitoring and threat hunting are vital components of advanced adversary detection. Rather than relying solely on automated systems, skilled threat hunters actively search for signs of adversaries within an organization's network. Threat hunters analyze network traffic, logs, and endpoint data to identify subtle indicators of compromise (IOCs). This proactive approach enables organizations to detect adversaries early in the attack lifecycle, potentially minimizing the damage caused.

Machine learning and artificial intelligence (AI) play a pivotal role in advanced adversary detection. These technologies can analyze vast datasets and identify patterns that are difficult for humans to discern. Machine learning models can be trained to recognize known adversary TTPs, enabling them to detect similar patterns in real-time data. As adversaries evolve, machine learning models can adapt to new tactics and behaviors, providing a dynamic defense mechanism.

Indicators of compromise (IOCs) and tactics, techniques, and procedures (TTPs) are critical components in advanced adversary detection. IOCs are specific artifacts or evidence of an adversary's presence, such as IP addresses, file hashes, or patterns of behavior. TTPs are broader, encompassing the methods and strategies adversaries use to achieve their objectives. By continually updating and sharing IOCs and TTPs with the broader cybersecurity community, organizations can benefit from collective intelligence to detect and respond to advanced threats more effectively.

Threat intelligence feeds are another valuable resource in advanced adversary detection. These feeds provide organizations with real-time information about emerging threats, including indicators of compromise and adversary TTPs. By integrating threat intelligence feeds into their security infrastructure, organizations can enhance their ability to detect and respond to advanced adversaries promptly.

Endpoint detection and response (EDR) solutions have gained prominence in the fight against advanced adversaries. These solutions provide real-time monitoring of endpoint devices, allowing security teams to detect suspicious activities, isolate compromised devices, and respond to incidents swiftly. EDR solutions can also collect and analyze endpoint data to identify IOCs and adversary behavior patterns.

Cloud-based security platforms are increasingly essential for organizations that rely on cloud services and infrastructure. These platforms offer advanced adversary detection capabilities tailored to cloud environments. They can monitor cloud-native services, analyze cloud logs, and detect deviations from established baselines. As more organizations migrate to the cloud, the integration of cloud-based security solutions becomes imperative for comprehensive adversary detection.

Intrusion detection systems (IDS) and intrusion prevention systems (IPS) have evolved to combat advanced adversaries effectively. These systems leverage signatures, behavioral analysis, and anomaly detection to identify suspicious network traffic and activities. When potential threats are detected, IDS and IPS can take automated actions to block or contain adversaries, limiting their impact.

Advanced adversary detection is an ongoing and collaborative effort. Cybersecurity professionals and organizations must remain vigilant, continuously updating their skills, tools, and strategies to stay ahead of adversaries. Threat intelligence sharing, industry partnerships, and information exchange forums play a crucial role in collectively defending against advanced threats.

In summary, the field of advanced adversary detection is rapidly evolving to counter the increasingly sophisticated tactics employed by threat actors. Through the integration of advanced technologies, proactive threat hunting, threat intelligence feeds, and collaborative efforts, organizations can bolster their defenses and effectively identify and respond to advanced adversaries before they inflict substantial damage. Adversary detection is not a one-size-fits-all endeavor; instead, it requires a multifaceted and adaptable approach to protect digital assets effectively.

In the realm of cybersecurity, one of the most critical components of an organization's defense strategy is a comprehensive incident response plan. Such a plan serves as a structured and proactive approach to dealing with security incidents, breaches, and threats to an organization's digital assets. It's not a matter of if, but when, an organization will face a security incident, making the development of a robust incident response plan a necessity.

At the heart of a comprehensive incident response plan is the understanding that cybersecurity incidents can encompass a wide range of scenarios, from malware infections and data breaches to denial-of-service attacks and insider threats. Each of these incidents requires a unique approach and predefined actions to mitigate their impact and prevent further harm.

To begin building a comprehensive incident response plan, it's crucial to establish clear objectives and priorities. These objectives should align with the organization's overall business goals and risk tolerance. Understanding what needs to be protected and the potential impact of various incidents helps in setting the right priorities for incident response.

The incident response team plays a central role in any plan. This team consists of individuals with specialized skills and responsibilities, including incident coordinators, investigators, analysts, and communicators. Their roles and responsibilities should be well-defined and understood to ensure a coordinated and efficient response.

Incorporating a well-defined incident categorization and severity assessment system is another essential aspect of a comprehensive incident response plan. This system allows the team to quickly assess the nature and severity of an incident, helping them allocate resources and prioritize actions accordingly. A standardized system ensures consistency in evaluating incidents.

One of the cornerstones of incident response planning is having a well-documented and communicated incident response policy. This policy outlines the organization's stance on cybersecurity incidents, defines the roles and responsibilities of the incident response team, and establishes the chain of command for incident handling. It also outlines the reporting process, ensuring that incidents are reported promptly to the appropriate personnel.

Another critical component of a comprehensive incident response plan is the creation of an incident response playbook. This playbook contains detailed, step-by-step procedures for responding to specific types of incidents. It serves as a practical guide for the incident response team, allowing them to execute predefined actions efficiently and effectively. The playbook should cover various scenarios, from malware outbreaks to data breaches, and should be updated regularly to reflect the evolving threat landscape.

Incident detection and notification are fundamental aspects of incident response. Organizations must have the necessary tools and systems in place to detect incidents promptly. This may include intrusion detection systems (IDS), security information and event management (SIEM) solutions, and endpoint detection and response (EDR) tools. When an incident is detected, it must be reported to the incident response team promptly.

Effective communication is a linchpin of incident response. It is essential to establish clear communication channels both within the incident response team and with external stakeholders, including senior management, legal counsel, law enforcement, and regulatory bodies. Transparency in communication is crucial to maintain trust and manage the public relations aspects of an incident.

As part of the plan, organizations should conduct regular incident response exercises and simulations. These exercises help the incident response team familiarize themselves with the procedures outlined in the playbook and identify areas for improvement. By simulating real-world scenarios, the team can refine their skills and response capabilities.

When an incident occurs, a crucial aspect of the plan is the containment and eradication of the threat. The incident response team must act swiftly to isolate affected systems, stop the attacker's access, and remove any malicious code or unauthorized access points. This phase aims to prevent further damage and maintain the integrity of the organization's digital assets.

Forensic analysis and evidence collection are also vital components of incident response. By conducting a thorough investigation, organizations can determine the scope and impact of the incident, identify the root cause, and gather evidence for potential legal actions. The ability to attribute the incident to a specific attacker or group is valuable for law enforcement and future prevention efforts.

After an incident is contained, eradicated, and investigated, the next steps involve recovery and remediation. This phase includes restoring affected systems to normal operation, implementing additional security measures to prevent similar incidents, and evaluating the organization's incident response performance to identify areas for improvement.

Continuous improvement is a fundamental principle in incident response planning. Organizations should conduct post-incident reviews to assess the effectiveness of their response, identify lessons learned, and update their incident response plan and playbook accordingly. This iterative process ensures that the organization becomes more resilient and better prepared to face future incidents.

In summary, a comprehensive incident response plan is an indispensable component of an organization's cybersecurity strategy. It provides a structured and coordinated approach to managing security incidents, from detection and notification to containment, eradication, recovery, and remediation. By investing in incident response planning and fostering a culture of preparedness, organizations can mitigate the impact of cybersecurity incidents and better protect their digital assets and reputation. Building and maintaining such a plan is an ongoing effort that requires dedication, expertise, and a commitment to continuous improvement in the face of an ever-changing threat landscape.

Chapter 10: Strategic Incident Response Planning and Execution

In the intricate realm of cybersecurity and incident response, the execution and coordination of efforts are the linchpins that hold the entire process together. When a security incident occurs, whether it's a data breach, malware infection, or a sophisticated cyberattack, the ability to respond swiftly and effectively is paramount. In this chapter, we'll delve into the critical aspects of executing and coordinating incident response efforts, shedding light on the intricate dance that occurs behind the scenes when a security incident unfolds.

Picture this scenario: An organization's security operations center (SOC) detects unusual activity on its network. Alarms are blaring, alerts are popping up on screens, and the incident response team springs into action. The first step is often a quick assessment of the situation. Is this a false positive, or is it a genuine incident that requires immediate attention? This initial assessment sets the stage for what comes next.

Once the incident response team confirms that an incident is indeed occurring, they must rapidly coordinate their efforts. This entails bringing together various members of the team, each with their own specialized skills and roles. Incident coordinators take charge, ensuring that everyone knows their responsibilities and that the incident is managed efficiently. The incident commander, often a senior member of the team, provides overall guidance and decisions on how to proceed.

Coordination extends beyond the incident response team itself. It involves liaising with other departments within the organization, such as legal, public relations, and executive management. These stakeholders need to be kept informed about the incident's progress, its potential impact on the organization, and the steps being taken to mitigate it. Effective communication is key, not only within the team but also with external parties.

Now, let's talk about containment. When dealing with a security incident, containment is often the first priority. The goal is to prevent the incident from spreading further and causing additional damage. This might involve isolating affected systems, blocking malicious network traffic, or shutting down compromised accounts. The incident response team must act decisively to contain the threat while minimizing disruptions to normal business operations.

As containment efforts progress, the incident response team simultaneously begins the process of eradication. Eradication is about permanently removing the threat from the environment. This could mean removing malware from infected systems, closing vulnerabilities that were exploited, or revoking unauthorized access. Eradication efforts must be methodical to ensure that the threat is completely eliminated, leaving no remnants behind.

Simultaneously, there's another critical aspect to consider: recovery. Once the incident is under control, the organization must work towards returning to normal operations. This involves restoring affected systems, services, and data to their pre-incident state. Depending on the nature of the incident, this can be a complex and time-consuming process. The incident response team must carefully plan and execute the recovery phase, ensuring that systems are not only functional but also secure.

Throughout these phases—containment, eradication, and recovery—documentation is essential. Detailed records of every action taken, every decision made, and every piece of evidence collected are vital. These records serve multiple purposes. They provide a clear trail of what happened during the incident, which can be invaluable for forensic analysis, legal proceedings, and post-incident reviews. They also aid in the reporting of the incident to relevant authorities and regulatory bodies.

Speaking of forensic analysis, it's a crucial part of the incident response process. Once the incident is contained and the immediate threats are addressed, investigators delve into the nitty-gritty details. They aim to understand how the incident occurred, what data or systems were affected, and who or what was responsible. Forensic analysis involves sifting through logs, examining network traffic, and studying the malware or attack vectors used. It's a painstaking process that requires a keen eye for detail.

But incident response doesn't end with forensic analysis. The next phase is an important one: reviewing and revising. Post-incident reviews are a chance for the incident response team to assess what went well and what could be improved. Were there any bottlenecks or delays in the response process? Were there tools or procedures that could have been more effective? The lessons learned from these reviews feed back into the organization's incident response plan and playbook, making it stronger and more agile for future incidents.

In parallel with all these efforts, there's an overarching theme: communication. Clear and consistent communication is essential throughout the incident response process. Internally, the incident response team must keep each other informed and aligned. Externally, the organization must communicate with stakeholders, partners, and possibly the public, depending on the nature and severity of the incident. Transparency builds trust, and the way an organization handles an incident can have a significant impact on its reputation.

Throughout this chapter, we've explored the intricacies of executing and coordinating incident response efforts. It's a dynamic and multifaceted process that requires a blend of technical expertise, communication skills, and a structured approach. When done effectively, incident response can mean the difference between a minor disruption and a full-blown crisis for an organization. It's a testament to the importance of preparedness and the ability to adapt swiftly in the ever-evolving landscape of cybersecurity threats.

Conclusion

In the world of cybersecurity, where threats evolve at an unprecedented pace, knowledge and preparedness are the keys to staying one step ahead of adversaries. The book bundle "Malware Analysis, Digital Forensics, and Cybersecurity Incident Response" has been a comprehensive journey through the intricate web of cyber threats and the robust defenses needed to protect our digital world. In Book 1, "Introduction to Malware Analysis and Digital Forensics for Cybersecurity," we set the stage, laying the foundation for understanding the complex ecosystem of malware and the critical role of digital forensics in uncovering its secrets. We explored the basics of malware types, their behavior, and the forensic techniques used to dissect them, providing readers with a solid understanding of the core concepts. Book 2, "Malware Detection and Analysis in Cybersecurity: A Practical Approach," delved deeper into the practical aspects of identifying, analyzing, and mitigating malware threats. We explored various malware detection approaches, from signature-based to heuristic and behavioral analysis. Armed with this knowledge, readers gained the skills needed to detect and respond effectively to evolving malware threats. In Book 3, "Advanced Cybersecurity Threat Analysis and Incident Response," we entered the realm of advanced cyber threats. We examined the tactics and techniques used by sophisticated adversaries, understanding the importance of threat intelligence and proactive threat hunting. This book elevated readers' capabilities, preparing them to face the ever-evolving landscape of cyber threats head-on. Finally, Book 4, "Expert Malware Analysis and Digital Forensics: Mastering Cybersecurity Incident Response," took our readers to the expert level. We explored in-depth malware analysis, memory forensics, and the intricacies of incident response. Armed with this knowledge, readers became masters in the art of dissecting malware and responding effectively to security incidents. Throughout this journey, we emphasized the critical role of collaboration and communication in the world of cybersecurity. Effective teamwork, both within organizations and across the cybersecurity community, is essential to combatting cyber threats.

As we conclude this book bundle, we hope that readers have gained a profound understanding of the intricate world of malware analysis, digital forensics, and incident response. The knowledge and skills acquired in these pages are not only invaluable but also essential in our digital age. Cyber threats will continue to evolve, and the defenders of cyberspace must evolve with them. With the knowledge and insights from this book bundle, readers are well-equipped to face the challenges of today and the uncertainties of tomorrow in the ever-changing landscape of cybersecurity. Remember, in the world of cyber threats, vigilance, adaptability, and a commitment to learning are your greatest allies. Stay curious, stay informed, and stay secure.

About Rob Botwright

Rob Botwright is a seasoned IT professional with a passion for technology and a career spanning over two decades. His journey into the world of information technology began with an insatiable curiosity about computers and a desire to unravel their inner workings. With a relentless drive for knowledge, he has honed his skills and expertise, becoming a respected figure in the IT industry.

Rob's fascination with technology started at a young age when he disassembled his first computer to understand how it operated. This early curiosity led him to pursue a formal education in computer science, where he delved deep into the intricacies of software development, network architecture, and cybersecurity. Throughout his academic journey, Rob consistently demonstrated an exceptional aptitude for problem-solving and innovation.

After completing his formal education, Rob embarked on a professional career that would see him working with some of the most renowned tech companies in the world. He has held various roles in IT, from software engineer to network administrator, and has been instrumental in implementing cutting-edge solutions that have streamlined operations and enhanced security for businesses of all sizes.

Rob's contributions to the IT community extend beyond his work in the corporate sector. He is a prolific writer and has authored numerous articles, blogs, and whitepapers on emerging technologies, cybersecurity best practices, and the ever-evolving landscape of information technology. His ability to distill complex technical concepts into easily understandable insights has earned him a dedicated following of readers eager to stay at the forefront of IT trends.

In addition to his writing, Rob is a sought-after speaker at industry conferences and seminars, where he shares his expertise and experiences with fellow IT professionals. He is known for his engaging and informative presentations, which inspire others to embrace innovation and adapt to the rapidly changing IT landscape.

Beyond the world of technology, Rob is a dedicated mentor who is passionate about nurturing the next generation of IT talent. He believes in the power of education and actively participates in initiatives aimed at bridging the digital divide, ensuring that young minds have access to the tools and knowledge needed to thrive in the digital age.

When he's not immersed in the realm of IT, Rob enjoys exploring the great outdoors, where he finds inspiration and balance. Whether he's hiking through rugged terrain or embarking on a new adventure, he approaches life with the same inquisitiveness and determination that have driven his success in the world of technology.

Rob Botwright's journey through the ever-evolving landscape of information technology is a testament to his unwavering commitment to innovation, education, and the pursuit of excellence. His passion for technology and dedication to sharing his knowledge have made him a respected authority in the field and a source of inspiration for IT professionals around the world.